New Approaches to the Personhood in Law

Tomasz Pietrzykowski / Brunello Stancioli (eds.)

New Approaches to the Personhood in Law

Essays in Legal Philosophy

PETER LANG
EDITION

Bibliographic Information published by the Deutsche Nationalbibliothek
The Deutsche Nationalbibliothek lists this publication in the Deutsche Nationalbibliografie; detailed bibliographic data is available in the internet at http://dnb.d-nb.de.

Library of Congress Cataloging-in-Publication Data
Names: Pietrzykowski, Tomasz, editor. | Stancioli, Brunello Souza, editor.
Title: New approaches to the personhood in law : essays in legal philosophy / Tomasz Pietrzykowski, Brunello Stancioli (eds.).
Description: Frankfurt am Main : Peter Lang, 2016.
Identifiers: LCCN 2015047339 | ISBN 9783631656853
Subjects: LCSH: Personality (Law) | Law—Philosophy.
Classification: LCC K627 .N49 2016 | DDC 340/.1—dc23 LC record available at http://lccn.loc.gov/2015047339

Cover illustration courtesy of Benjamin Ben Chaim

This publication was financially supported by the University of Silesia.

ISBN 978-3-631-65685-3 (Print)
E-ISBN 978-3-653-05054-7 (E-Book)
DOI 10.3726/978-3-653-05054-7

Peter Lang Edition is an Imprint of Peter Lang GmbH.

Peter Lang – Frankfurt am Main · Bern · Bruxelles · New York · Oxford · Warszawa · Wien

This publication has been peer reviewed.

www.peterlang.com

Contents

Tomasz Pietrzykowski and Brunello Stancioli

Introduction: Modern Challenges to the Concept of a Person in Law

At first sight it may seem that the legal language offers few concepts that are clearer and simpler than a person in law. It is used on a daily basis in statutes, rulings, treatises and textbooks in numerous fields of law and usually does not stir controversies. It suggests that at least its core meaning has to remain the subject of a widespread consensus within respective legal communities. There are some well-known problems but they concern rather borderline cases, such as the status of a human fetus, anencephalic newborns or – more recently – pre-implanted embryos created in the process of in-vitro fertilization. In reality, however, there are few concepts in the present legal vocabulary that are more vulnerable to revolutionary changes brought by the ethical debates following the advancements of science and technology. Many strands of the contemporary developments in biological, medical or computer sciences may present a challenge to our idea of personhood as an important part of conceptual and ethical assumptions underlying legal systems. Its potential consequences may profoundly affect the way in which the whole legal system is conceived, including practically all fields of legal regulation.

In contemporary legal thought we are used to regard a person in law as either a human being (whichever moments are specified as the beginning and the end of her legally recognized status) or organizational entities designated by the law as separate rights-holders – corporations, states, municipalities, churches and the like. On the other hand, everything that is not a person, the law considers as a kind of objects or things (with minor exceptions for such phenomena as energy, water or air that hardly fit the conceptual criteria of being a "thing"). In other words, one may be either a subject or a party of legal relations (a person) or merely their object (a thing). In this way, the legal distinction between *personae* and *rei* somehow mirrors the deeper and more general dichotomy of a subject and an object, permeating not only philosophical but also ordinary, commonsense thinking.

The dualist distinction between persons and things is well rooted in the history of legal thought and originated at least in the ideas conceived by Roman jurists. Nonetheless, it would be a serious mistake to assume that the meaning and scope of legal personhood, as we know it today, have been a stable and unchanging ingredient of the legal conceptualization of reality. On the contrary, it has gone through profound evolution making the contemporary legal concept of a person essentially different than it used to be in the past. For centuries, legal systems by no means recognized each and every human being as a person in law. What the legal language today refers to as a "natural" personhood of human beings was denied to large groups of people, such as slaves, newborns before their acceptance by their father, women, captives, non-citizens or convicts punished with the so-called civil-death penalty (such as *bannitio* in many old European laws) or declared "enemy of the Roman people" in the ancient Roman law.

So-called juristic personhood of organizational entities was even more historically contingent and varied depending on the local conditions of the given time and place. The very idea of a separate legal personhood emerged in late Roman law and was theoretically developed mainly by medieval canonists. Its point was to let some collective bodies such as e.g. church or religious orders act on its own behalf and be able to acquire and hold rights and duties legally detached from those belonging to particular individuals involved into its operations. Later on, however, it became one of the crucial legal tools facilitating the rapid development of market economy, massive industrial and commercial activities and the general social structure.

Due to its practical significance, the concept of juristic personhood has attracted enormous interests of the 19th century legal scholarship, passionately debating the "nature" of such a person. Those debates have yielded a considerable number of competing theories, identifying juristic personhood either with a pure conceptual fiction or with a real entity, the actual substrate of which is a collective of people, their common will or shared property appropriated to pursue their goals. Nowadays, however, the interest in the general theory of juristic personhood has been gradually overshadowed by controversies concerning the scope and kinds of rights the organizational entities may and should be attributed. Every now and then, some disputable legal cases reinvigorate these controversies. An excellent recent example may be the famous Hobby Lobby case, in which the US Supreme Court was confronted with the question whether commercial companies, as juristic persons, hold constitutionally protected freedom of conscience (the Supreme Court answered in the affirmative).

However, setting historical details aside, one may say in a nutshell that the debates on the natural personhood focused mainly on the extension of the concept (namely, at which moment of biological existence of a human organism its recognition as a legal person should begin and end), while in respect of juristic personhood – they concerned mainly the intension (an essence or point) of the concept of juristic person. Out of those developments of both legal thought and legal regulations emerged the modern conceptual framework of legal personhood consisting of recognition of each human being from birth to death (defined as irreversible loss of brain or cardiac activity) as a natural persons in law and some range of private and public organizational entities as artificial juristic persons. This approach to personhood in law has become, however, the subject of a widespread (even if rough and sometimes only declaratory) consensus relatively recently. Hence, it would be a serious mistake to take it as an eternal and inescapable foundation of any conceivable legal order.

The lesson we propose to learn from such wider historical perspective is a deep skepticism over the belief that the concept of a person in law has in our times reached the end of its evolution and our current conceptual determinations are ultimate "one right answers" to all questions concerning legal recognition of personhood. Perhaps each epoch is tempted to consider its own basic moral and philosophical convictions as eventual approximations to the truth after the mistakes and superstitions of the past generations have been finally debunked. One of the guiding tacit assumptions of this book is the advice that we should be wary not to fall prey of this natural illusion making it difficult to notice and admit the contingency of our apparently self-evident suppositions. It would be utterly naïve to believe that our understanding of what it means to be person and how it should be reflected in the law will remain unchanged in the next fifty, hundred or two hundred years. Arguably, in view of the problems and perplexities of the idea of a person that may be identified even today, just by sheer examination of the current state of the scientific and philosophical discussions, such belief could be even qualified as more than utterly naïve.

The combined significance of the wide range of such problems and perplexities is rapidly growing. Biological sciences prove evolutionary continuity of consciousness and the presence of complex affective and cognitive processes in the minds of many non-human animals. It poses compelling questions of the proper legal status of non-human sentient creatures that until recently has been almost universally regarded as mere things. In recent years the claims for personification of at least some highly developed animals (such as chimpanzees or dolphins) have been noticeably transforming from the problem discussed by a bunch of radical philosophers into the question visiting parliamentary chambers and legal courtrooms.

Bioengineers are advancing technologies of creating organisms composed of genetic or cellular material derived from creatures of two different species. As a consequence many examples of viable inter-species biological chimeras or hybrids have been manufactured, including animals with mixed brain structures. Relatively limited scope of application of these technologies to create human-animal mixtures results more from ethical objections and developing legal constraints than purely biological obstacles. Nonetheless, some remarkable experimental results strongly suggest that, as a matter of principle, creating various kinds of human-animal chimeras and hybrids is attainable (even if many technical difficulties would have to be solved in an extensive experimental efforts). Irrespective of whether it will ever actually happen (to say nothing about whether it should ever happen), even today animals with admixed portions of human genome or tissue (including populations of neural cells) no longer belong to hypothetical Sci-Fi scenarios and became reality of many scientific laboratories all over the world. Arguably, it casts some fundamental doubts on the traditional criteria of human "natural" personhood that assume that there is a clear-cut, unbridgeable gap between human and non-human organisms (and consequently linking species-membership with the moral and legal status). It is not difficult to notice that the existing criteria of natural personhood are hardly reconcilable with the perspective of creating organisms of mixed human-animal genetic and phenotypical composition.

Similar concerns seem to follow from another strand of research, that is, manufacturing of increasingly autonomous software agents and humanoid robots. The advancement of these technologies has been initially driven mainly by military purposes but today some promising consumer market opportunities for such devices have been also found (software bots, autonomous cars, robots accompanying and caring for the elderly patients etc.). It may mean that the years of a slow-down in the artificial intelligence research, partially due to the limited funding related to unclear dedication of potential inventions, is now over. This, in turn, may lead to the revival of the old questions of the status that such autonomous intelligent objects should occupy (and the criteria applicable to establish it). The questions that in this context would belong more to the domain of practical legislative or judicial dilemmas than traditional, pure philosophical speculation.

Our settled criteria of personhood are gradually undermined also by the growth of biomedical technologies of replacement defective parts of human organism by artificial devices. Various stages of research include wide variety of medical appliances – ranging from artificial internal organs such as heart or lungs, through systems aiming to substitute damaged sensory channels (such as artificial retina, up to the brain chips designed to prevent or recover from neurological dysfunctions (as e.g. artificial hippocampus hoped to combat memory loss). Another promising area of biomedical inventions involves brain interfaces that should let the patient control an external equipment directly by thought. All these developments may have important consequences for the way in which human bodies and brains will continue to become closer and closer integrated with artificial equipment improving their natural capacities. The further such integration proceeds inside human organism, the more doubts it casts on the humanness as the key criterion to count as a "natural" (nomen omen) person.

The problem of what is a "person" is no longer an "a priori" matter, it is about the person's construction and self-construction. Many problems will arise from this change. The creation of *in vitro* brain tissue and the interfaces of this tissue with silicon platforms might originate hybrid beings (organic and inorganic) which might have all the requirements to be persons – such as self-conscience, memory, practical reasoning, and values. And yet they might not be entirely made of DNA and carbon based cells.

The status of these new entities will no longer be connected to their biophysical constitution. It will be defined by ethics and law. In the assessment of what is a person, the capacity of action, interaction and recognition, identity and feeling of belonging will substitute traditional elements such as body, genetic material, soul, religion or "human nature."

This book aims to address at least some of the problems daunting the idea of personhood nowadays. Taking into account the importance of their potential moral and legal implications we find it compelling to confront them from the perspective of legal theory and philosophy of law. It is this part of legal scholarship that should notice and examine the conceptual and ethical challenges for the law before they have to be solved by judges and legislators. We hope that the problems and perspectives discussed in the papers collected in this volume give a clear clue of what those challenges may be as well as of how profound and far-reaching they may actually turn out. This is what we regard as the main value and the common message of all topics discussed in the following chapters, devoted to closer inspection of many aspects of the present approach to the personhood in law as well as imminent challenges it will have to face in the years to come.

Ethics and law will be the transdisciplinary medium for the definition of our subjects of law. Free from theological (*imago Dei*) and biological (*DNA*) biases, the legal discourse embedded in everyday life will enable possibilities for the reconstruction of the "natural persons" in different basis.

To be whomever they want lies in the hands of the persons themselves. In the long way we have come from Mirandola until today the person is now, more than ever, "the *free and sovereign artificer* of thyself."

This book has been prepared and published with financial support of the Polish National Center of Science (project 2012/07/B/HS5/03957)

Tomasz Pietrzykowski

Law, Personhood, and the Discontents of Juridical Humanism*

1. The Legal Approach to Personhood

According to the standard legal account of personhood, a person is defined as an entity capable of holding rights and duties. The status of a person in law is conferred by the law itself; therefore, the choices of the particular lawmakers determine to whom legal rights and duties might be ascribed. The law traditionally distinguishes between two separate kinds of persons. Natural or physical persons include human beings, while so-called legal persons refer to various organizational entities, such as corporations, associations, states, and municipalities. The range of entities to which particular jurisdictions grant personhood vary in time and place. In particular, for the majority of the history of law, numerous groups of people, such as slaves, women, and children, were refused full recognition as independent rights holders and were practically reduced to the category of property or objects of the unlimited power of others.

Thus, at first sight, it may seem that the legal approach to personhood does not follow the philosophical tradition, which primarily identifies personhood with rational agency. As the famous early medieval thinker Boetius put it, the person is conceived mainly as *rationalis naturae individua substantia*. Later on, personhood became associated with the ability to make a conscious self-determination, which was typical for mature, normally developed human beings. All that seems rather distant from the above conceptualization of personhood that is operative in the legal discourse.

I shall argue, however, that such a view—that is, one that sharply distinguishes between the legal and philosophical accounts of personhood—is superficial and, at least partially, incorrect. Unquestionably, the status of a person in law involves a strong element of conventionality. It is true that the lawmaker has the power to formally confer or deny the status of rights holder to such an array of entities as he pleases. However, this is by no means the whole story. What the law says and what lawmakers do always rely on certain assumptions about the nature and structure

* This paper has been prepared for the research project financed by the Polish National Center of Science (2012/07/B/HS5/03957).

of reality, its meaning and value, and the role and ends of the law itself. One may say, then, that legal rules necessarily reflect a certain philosophy without which their content would not make much sense. A complete set of the philosophical assumptions that underlie the rules of law is rarely directly or unequivocally articulated anywhere in legal texts. Rather, such assumptions are manifested in the content and practice of law and remain part of a given legal culture in which the institutional arrangements of law are embedded. Hence, their identification requires a deliberate analytical effort that extends beyond—or rather below—the normative level of legal texts and technical legal terms.

2. Juridical Humanism

The philosophical assumptions of a legal system include some that concern the approach to personhood. They determine whose interests should matter in law and why. The existence of such assumptions guides and explains the normative regulations of personhood on the level of legal rules. I am of the opinion that one of the key philosophical foundations of the contemporary legal order is the belief that the law ultimately serves to promote human good and that the community of law is actually composed of all but only human beings.[1] I would call this view the "Juridical Humanism Thesis." It relies on the concept of inherent human dignity resulting from the uniquely human capabilities of rational thinking and decision-making. Therefore, the sole fact of being human is considered the only precondition of having interests relevant to law and of deserving by their holder to be recognized as a being entitled to legal protection for his or her own sake. This implies a belief in an objectively ascertainable essential gap between humans and the rest of the world. Humans are believed to be so different from any other kinds of creatures that the law is morally justified to regard the human good as the principal concern and supreme objective of the legal system. In this sense, Juridical Humanism seems to be based on a rather strong version of human exceptionalism.

Based on the aforementioned view, there appears to be an essential difference between the nature of personhood attributed by law to human beings and the one it confers on organizational entities. The recognition of the latter as separate holders of rights and duties is derivative and based on essentially pragmatic grounds. Namely, it is supposed to serve as a tool to better realize some human needs and interests. The ultimate, noninstrumental end of the recognition of any

1 This kind of recognition seems to be postulated by Article 6 of the Universal Declaration of Human Rights, which proclaims that "everyone has the right to recognition as a person before the law."

organizational entity is the promotion of human flourishing. Even in Ancient Rome, where the separate personhood of collective bodies originated, eminent lawyers emphasized that, as famous lawyer Hermogenianus put it, *hominem causa ius omnes constitutum est.*[2] This principle, together with the idea of the inherent dignity and equal value of all human beings, is the essence of contemporary Juridical Humanism.

3. Contemporary Science and the Decline of Human Exceptionalism

Some of the advances in contemporary science and technology bring about growing difficulties for Juridical Humanism. They seem to overshadow the old and commonly known perplexities with which Juridical Humanism has been coping for a long time, such as the disputable status of human embryos, anencephalic infants, or patients in a persistent vegetative state. New, deeper, and potentially more devastating challenges for the ethical defensibility of Juridical Humanism include the status of higher animals, human–animal biological mixtures, the cyborgization of the human body and brain, as well as the development of artificial autonomous agents. These seem to erode Juridical Humanism and may finally put it in a serious crisis. The idea that some strands of contemporary scientific and technological progress pose a serious threat to the very foundations of the existing philosophical basis for the legal account of personhood I will call the "Juridical Humanism Decline Thesis." Its essential point is the claim that some implications of the discoveries and inventions of our times undermine the belief in human exceptionalism being the backbone of the modern legal approach to personhood.

Animals, including those with highly developed, complex nervous systems, have been traditionally regarded by the law as mere things. Since they belong to a nonhuman biological species, human exceptionalism automatically excludes all of them from the community of persons. Moreover, due to the fact that the law traditionally distinguishes only between persons and things, it follows that all animals must be qualified as objects to which the rules related to property are applicable. In view of the discoveries in the ethology, evolutionary biology, and cognitive sciences of the previous two centuries, such treatment of animals must seem more and more ethically problematic. There can no longer be any reasonable doubt that many species of animals (in particular, vertebrates such as mammals or birds) are able to experience complex conscious states, including pain, fear, joy,

2 Digesta, 1.5.2 (quote from Codex Hermogenianus).

loneliness, longing, sorrow, and so forth. In respect of the capabilities of animal minds, it research proves that there is actually no human capacity that would not, at least to some degree, also be present among animals, including some rudimentary forms of phenomena such as morality, culture, or normativity (see for example Pietrzykowski, 2007, 123ff.). Moreover, for any single feature that could be potentially contemplated as distinctly human, there are at least some animals that exhibit it to a higher degree than at least some human beings (which is the basis of the so-called "marginal cases" argument against human exceptionalism).

Research on animals, which gradually uncovers the complexity of their minds, is accompanied by an increasing awareness of the evolutionary continuity that exists between human and nonhuman animals. This is followed by creeping changes in social attitudes, which, in some legal systems, resulted in the so-called dereification of higher animals. This technical term refers to the formal exclusion of animals from the legal category of things.[3] Nowhere in the world, however, was such an operation meant as granting animals any form of personhood.[4] In this way, animals became, in a sense, "stuck" somewhere in between, being neither objects nor subjects of the law. As a consequence, in many cases, they occupy a position that is hardly consistent with the standard conceptual framework of the legal thinking, which, from Roman times, has divided reality principally into three categories: persons, things, and actions.[5]

---

3 In one case (at least, this is one such case with which I am familiar), Swiss law began to recognize the dignity of the animal being. Art. 120. 2 [concerning genetic technologies] reads: "*Der Bund erlässt Vorschriften über den Umgang mit Keim- und Erbgut von Tieren, Pflanzen und anderen Organismen. Er trägt dabei der Würde der Kreatur sowie der Sicherheit von Mensch, Tier und Umwelt Rechnung und schützt die genetische Vielfalt der Tier- und Pflanzenarten*". In Art. 1 of the Swiss Animal Protection Law of 2005, it is stated even more clearly that "*Zweck dieses Gesetzes ist es, die Würde und das Wohlergehen des Tieres zu schützen.*"

4 This is despite recurring, though unsuccessful, attempts, such as legal actions for the Hiasl chimpanzee in Austria, Steven Wise's Nonhuman Rights Project, and the Great Ape Project initiatives in several countries (e.g., Spain). However, some changes in law make their situation increasingly closer to quasi-personal status despite the refusal to confer them any kind of formal personhood; one example may be the almost unconditional ban on the use of great apes in experiments, which came into force in European Union law in 2013.

5 This division stems from Roman law, according to the famous formula by Gaius: "*Omne autem ius, quo utimur, vel ad personas pertinet vel ad res vel ad actiones*" (Gaius, Institutiones, 1.II.8).

The second considerable problem for Juridical Humanism arises from the biomedical research involving human–animal mixtures, which include, above all, interspecies chimeras and hybrids (for general review see Teupniz, Weschka 2009). A biological human–animal chimera is an organism in which human and animal cell populations are combined. Chimeras of this kind are created primarily by inserting human stem cells into animal embryos. It is supposed to be a means to breed human organs, such as the liver, heart, lungs, or stomach, in animal bodies so that they can serve patients who are awaiting transplantation surgery. In several cases, partially successful experiments related to the creation of human–animal chimeras involved transferring human brain cells to murine embryos, which later developed into animals with some portion of human neurons in their brains.[6] Conversely, interspecies hybrids are created by fusing portions of the genetic code of different biological origins. In some cases, interspecies hybrids may result from the ordinary sexual reproduction of animals belonging to closely related species. An example of this is a mule being a genetic combination of a donkey and a horse. The hybrid offspring of parents belonging to different species are typically infertile. The contemporary technologies of genetic engineering allow for the creation of a flexible genetic combination of a fertilized egg, giving rise to hybrids that are inaccessible by means of mere sexual intercourse. They include animals with some portions of genetic code of human origin, such as "humanized" mice (e.g., mice with genetic modifications making them develop humanlike immune system to model immunological reactions of a human organism). However, the outcomes that have been obtained to date are still rather far from the actual birth of a viable creature manifesting an externally noticeable mixture of human and animal morphological or behavioral traits. Numerous technical difficulties remain unsolved. Moreover, the experiments that may result with bringing such creatures into being evoke in most places in the world strong ethical objections and become subject of emerging legal restrictions.

Nonetheless, with regard to this research, the state of the art strongly suggests that biological human–animal mixtures are no longer only imagined, hypothetical entities that are known from purely speculative thought experiments but rather a matter of further progress in the already available techniques that are used in numerous laboratories all over the world. It renders insufficient the implicitly assumed genetic or morphological criteria of being human and, as such, of counting

6 The most famous experiments on human–animal neural chimeras have been performed by the team of Irving Weissman in Stanford and F. Gage in Salk Institute at La Jolla CA. (Greely *et al.* 2007; see also e.g. Muotri *et al.* 2005).

as a member of the community of law. Moreover, it undermines the belief in an objective, unbridgeable gap between the human and nonhuman worlds. In this way, Juridical Humanism is converted from one view—that the principal difference between human beings and other creatures justifies the privileged status of the former—into another view, according to which human beings should try to prevent any attempts to bridge that gap to ensure that their morally superior position remains unchallenged. Notably, such a reformulation makes Juridical Humanism a weak and ethically questionable standpoint.

The third significant issue for Juridical Humanism is a result of the technologies that aim to produce artificial devices to replace parts of human organisms as well as the progress in building wholly artificial agents that are capable of increasingly autonomous humanlike behavior and decision making. The technical enhancement of the defective parts of the human body is nothing new. We have already become accustomed to the idea of bionic arms, hearts, cochlear implants, retinas, and even tongues.[7] However, such technologies have now begun to expand to the domain of direct interventions into the mind. An example might be a currently tested chip to be implanted into the brain to stimulate the neural structures of the hippocampus in hopes of combating memory loss (e.g. Berger, Glanzman 2005; Hampson *et al.* 2013). The advances in implantable devices of this kind have revived the famous "ship of Theseus paradox"—namely the question of how many and which parts of the human organism may be replaced by their artificial equivalents without converting a human being into some other kind of entity.

The emerging technology of autonomous software and mobile agents creates similar problems from the opposite direction—how much similarity to living creatures (not necessarily humans) such machines have to exhibit to cast doubts on their status as mere programmed objects. Even today, the level of their complexity has already begun to pose some new regulatory questions regarding, for example, the liability for decisions taken by driverless cars, autonomous drones, and software-trading bots. Some argue that there will soon be considerable pragmatic reasons to grant a limited separate legal personhood to at least some of the most advanced artificial agents (Pagallo 2013, Chopra/White 2011, Solum 1992). In addition, some market and commercial opportunities suggest that the further development of the existing technologies may, in the near future, lead to at least semiautonomous companion agents dedicated to assist older or disabled people, take care of children, and help to perform certain jobs, not to mention

7 See, for example, http://www.livescience.com/11381-bionic-humans-top-10-technologies.html.

obvious military applications, and largely stimulating numerous subfields of the present research on artificially intelligent agents. Several machines of this kind existing today may serve as examples of the extremely primitive forerunners of such semiautonomous humanoids and give some impression of the direction in which this technology is heading.

Thus, even remaining skeptical in respect of the perspectives of any genuine, strong artificial intelligence, we have to at least take into account the presence of machines or software agents that perform complex tasks in an increasingly autonomous fashion by extending the scope of humanlike patterns of action and which are presumably able to trigger some emotional reactions in the people with whom they interact. We should remember that the computational power of each smartphone today exceeds that of the entire equipment used by the National Aeronautics and Space Administration to send the first people to the moon only decades ago. Similarly, in the coming years, commonly used personal devices may well have much greater capacities than those of today's most advanced humanoid robots or software agents, which are bestowed with the ability to navigate through the environment, recognize faces, react flexibly to and by voice communications, and even display artificial emotions or needs (as in the case of robots that are able to detect that they are running out of energy and react by looking for a source into which to plug themselves to reload; this closely resembles the hunger or thirst of a living creature). Primitive forms of these capacities are present in the existing machines—such as Honda's Asimo; Toyota's Partner or Robina; the Massachusetts Institute of Technology's Kismet, Nao, or Nexi; and the military autonomous machines created by the Defense Advanced Research Projects Agency—therefore, their further development seems anything but a "sci-fi scenario."

More than half a century ago, Alan Turing proposed his famous test for the evaluation of the artificial intelligence of a computer. A crucial idea that seems to lie behind the famous conversation-with-the-computer criterion seems to be the conviction (which I find unquestionably true) that our principal basis for ascribing sentience, intelligence, and internal experiences to other beings is an inference from the externally observable behavior of the latter (including, but not limited to, their verbal communications). These more basic claims could be called a generalized Turing test. An inclination to conceive certain behavioral patterns of others as revealing their goals or intentions seems to be one of our evolutionary adaptations, enabling us to more quickly and accurately predict the expected further course of their actions. This seems to have serious practical implications—namely, from a certain level of complexity, it may become difficult for people to suppress their natural disposition to attribute mental states to appropriately behaving machines.

Thus, in our attitudes toward autonomous agents, we may face a dilemma—we will either humanize them or dehumanize ourselves.

I have outlined three simultaneous processes—the development of knowledge about animals; biotechnological research on interspecies, human-animal, biological organisms; and the rise of technologies by which humanlike behavior may be realized by means of technical devices integrated with human flesh or even by entirely nonorganic agents. It is the convergence of these processes that may, in my opinion, mean serious hardship for human exceptionalism underpinning the special recognition currently granted by law to human beings and their interests.

The processes in question will be able to exert a practical influence on the institutional arrangements of law, however, only after their moral implications become sufficiently blatant and widespread in the popular worldview. These kinds of changes in social attitudes are rarely swift or sudden. In the past, coming to terms with the consequences of major scientific breakthroughs could have taken not years but rather decades or even centuries. However, time seems to have accelerated remarkably. In respect of personhood in law, the discussion might be additionally invigorated by practical problems that legal systems face and will perpetually continue to face. This perspective urges to not only address immediate regulatory issues but to also look ahead and scrutinize the more basic and far-reaching influence of the processes taking place these days regarding the tenability of our legal ideas and their deeper philosophical foundations.

4. Toward Necessary Conceptual Refinements

Perhaps it is too early to ascertain whether Juridical Humanism will finally be forced to collapse or only change to somehow accommodate the new phenomena in question. In any case, I am of the opinion that it will be unable to overcome the growing discrepancy between its main tenets and the external reality without serious refinements of its much-too-crude conceptual framework. I propose that we call this idea the "Necessity of Further Conceptual Distinctions Thesis."

There seem to be two main conceptual discriminations that legal thought evidently lacks. The first is a clear detachment between the concepts of a person and a human being. Theoretically, such a distinction is well known and is deeply rooted in legal thought; after all, some persons recognized by law are not human individuals but organizational entities. However, as I argued before, this is only superficially true. In fact, legal orders are based on the moral foundation of Juridical Humanism attributing substantial moral value solely to human beings and considering their good as the only proper objective of the institution of law. Now, for the first time, we have to admit the possibility of creatures in which humanlike—or better, person-like—qualities may be detected despite the fact that they do not meet the standard criteria of humanness. This renders obsolete the intuitive recognition that the membership of the human species is *the* criterion of the membership of the legal community. As a consequence, it becomes necessary to reconsider such criteria to grasp the idea of nonhuman or not-entirely human personhood.

Presumably, their amendment or improvement will turn out to be inherently controversial or unable to produce any clear-cut outcomes. Nonetheless, some conditions of being a person—at least partially independent of simply understood species membership—will have to be discussed and publicly agreed upon if the law is to be prepared to respond adequately to the practical problems resulting from the advancements of science and technology. However, for a number of reasons, I tend to endorse the view that any potential criteria of this kind should not apply to human beings, whom, as a matter of principle, should remain recognized as persons, at least to the same extent as today, without imposing any further species-independent conditions.

Nevertheless, there is another distinction, which I find even more compelling and urgently needed: The concept of a person should be, in my opinion, conspicuously decoupled from the concept of "subject-hood" (if I may propose such a term). By person, I mean someone having humanlike properties, making it plausible to confer legal rights on and hold him or her accountable for his or her actions. Lacking some of these properties, should not, however, entail an automatic relegation to the category of things. In other words, not being a person should not be identified with an inability to have any subjective interests that matter morally and deserve legal protection solely for their own sake.

There seems to be no rational reason why the law should continue to follow the ancient dichotomy of persons and things and thus keep lacking an intermediate category to capture those entities whose features fit neither the idea of persons nor of mere objects. This postulated category of nonpersonal subjects of law, as opposed to personhood, would not imply the ability to make intentional use of rights or to be held liable for the fulfillment of duties. Conversely, in distinction to objecthood, it would imply the capability to possess one's own subjective interests, the moral relevance of which may merit legal consideration. The point of the idea of nonpersonal subjects of law is granting them some level of legal protection not because of any interests of third persons (as it happens in respect of things having value for someone) but rather *against* any such interests.[8] The law should

8 Such detachment would usually require a constitutional amendment. The rough wording of such a provision could read as follows: "*1. [Irrespective of the protection of the*

protect nonpersonal subjects from arbitrary or unjustified violations of their own subjective interests adequate to the nature and scope of the interests to which they could be reasonably attributed and the extent to which the interests in question are not trumped by the competing rights or interests of others.

The most obvious candidates for this category are sentient animals and those human or partially human creatures that are, today, denied the status of a person and, therefore, are either deprived of any legal protection whatsoever or remain in a kind of a gray, undefined zone of uncertainty. They include the aforementioned embryos, anencephalic newborns, and some of the patients who are in a persistent vegetative state. I would like to emphasize, however, that the idea of nonpersonal subjects of law should be a means to elevate the status of the creatures that are currently excluded from the category of persons rather than to decrease the position of those who are now granted full personhood and enjoy corresponding legal respect.

5. Concluding Remarks

The above conceptual distinctions are, in my opinion, necessary, though vastly insufficient, elements of the unavoidable reconsideration of the philosophical basis of the legal approach to personhood. We cannot be sure how fast the ongoing developments in science and technology will prompt actual changes in the existing form of Juridical Humanism let alone in the respective institutional arrangements of particular legal systems. It would be naïve, however, to believe that time can be stopped and that the current philosophical foundations of the law will not continue to evolve. Perhaps each epoch is, to some extent, lured to see its own basic moral convictions as the ultimate wisdom finally overcoming the primitive superstitions held by previous generations. However, history teaches us that, in this respect, as Heraclitus famously put it many centuries ago, everything flows, and change is the only constant in life.

Surprisingly enough, science and technology force us to reexamine in the twenty-first century the same basic question posed in the gospel of Luke. Jesus was famously asked by a scholar of law "Who is my neighbor?" However, upon

fundamental rights of persons], the law protects the basic interests of each human creature and other subjects capable of holding the interests vital for the subjective quality of their existence, even if they are not persons according to the meaning of the law." The scope of such protection, means, and actions necessary to effectuate it as well as persons competent to make use of them on behalf of protected subjects shall be determined by the appropriate statutes.

closer inspection, this should not be at all surprising; it seems to be merely another reexamination of this eternal puzzle, which has already been examined numerous times in the past and will presumably be further reexamined countless other times in the future. Some people—especially lawyers—may feel a little uncomfortable dealing with issues that touch on the very essence of human self-understanding; after all, this is not the kind of problem with which lawyers deal on a daily basis. Yet, for even the most dogmatic lawyers, the refusal to draw consequences based on what is happening is not a reasonable policy for coping with reality.

References

Berger Theodore and Glanzman Dennis (2005): *Towards Replacement Parts of the Brain: Implantable Biomimetic Electronics as Neural Protheses*, Cambridge Mass.

Chopra Samir, White Laurence (2011): *A Legal Theory for Autonomous Artifical Agents*, Ann Arbor.

Dombrowski David (1997): *Babies and Beasts: The Argument from Marginal Cases*, Chicago.

Greely Henry *et al.* (2007): *Thinking about Human Neuron Mouse,* American Journal of Bioethics, 7 (5).

Hampson Robert *et al.* (2013): 'Facilitation of Memory Encoding in Primate Hippocampus by a Neuroprosthesis that Promotes Task-specific Neural Firing', *Journal of Neural Engineering* 10 (6).

Pagallo Ugo (2013): *The Laws of Robots*, Dordrecht.

Muotri Allyson *et al.* (2005): 'Development of functional human embryonic stem cell-derived neurons in mouse brain', *Proceedings of the National Academy of Sciences of the USA*, Vol. 102, No. 51; doi: 10.1073/pnas.0509315102.

Pietrzykowski Tomasz (2007): 'The Roots of Normativity: From Neuroscience to Legal Theory' In: J. Stelmach, W. Załuski, M. Soniewicka Eds. *Studies in the Philosophy of Law, Vol. 4. Legal Philosophy and the Challenge of Biosciences.* Krakow.

Solum Laurence (1992): 'Legal Personhood for Artificial Intelligences', *North Carolina Law Review*, Vol. 70.

Taupitz Jochen, Weschka, Marion (2009) Eds.: *Chimbrids. Chimeras and Hybrids in Comparative European and Interneational Research. Scientific, Ethical, Philosophical and Legal Aspects*, Dordrecht-Heidelberg-London-New York.

Brunello Stancioli and Daniel Ribeiro

Dignity as Constraint and as Freedom: On the Meanings of Human Dignity for a Transhuman World

1. Introduction

Addressing the de-construction and re-construction of the legal concept of a "natural person" is an issue that presents several philosophical and theoretical challenges. Of those challenges, perhaps one of the most enduring is the dilemma confronting any attempt to remove natural personhood from its firm ground in humanity.

Indeed, humanity, the state of being human, is inexorably linked to the legal status of being a person: having the legal capacity to act and engage in legal transactions, and being entitled to rights and protections under the law. However, the law also recognizes non-human beings as legal persons. Currently, this recognition extends only to certain social entities and institutions, organized and created to attend to human goals. These social entities and institutions are regarded as discrete legal subjects that make human collective action more effective, make it easier to ascribe liability for such actions and, ultimately, legally account for human social gregariousness. Thus, even non-human persons, as they exist in our current legal landscapes, are undeniably human or, rather, are an expression of humanity.

This scenario prompts the question: could there genuinely be non-human persons? Or, is personhood inextricably tied to humanity?

First, why are these questions important? The firm linkage between humanity and personhood has been responsible for assuring a continuous expansion of the moral circle of beings deserving of respect and equal treatment under the law. Historical processes that witnessed, for instance, black slaves in the Americas achieve equal civil rights or the gains in gender equality achieved by feminist movements in most Western societies are proof that affirming humanity has been an important means of claiming equal status under the law. Indeed, this equal status under the law means the recognition of a being as a person. Despite all the good that has come from it, the process of binding personhood to humanity has a more perverse side.

Humans have become somewhat too attached to their own exceptionalism and fearful of becoming something else. This moral fright has taken shape more sharply since the tremendous advances in scientific knowledge and techniques in genetic engineering and artificial intelligence, for instance, have enabled humans to conceivably "break away" from their own natures. The possibilities presented by genetic enhancements and artificial brains, to cite two of many examples, are daunting because they seem to meddle with the very fabric of what could be called "human nature".

In this chapter, a very specific trend in the arguments of those who attempt to defend humanity against the threat posed by modern technology will be explored: the usage of the concept of human dignity as a constraint to technological interventions applied for self-modification and enhancement and as a normative limit that entails respect for human nature and the human condition.

This trend can be exemplified by the reference to dignity in several international conventions and declarations of rights concerning bioethics at the end of the twentieth century and beginning of the twenty-first century. UNESCO's Universal Declaration on the Human Genome and Human Rights and Europe's Convention for the Protection of Human Rights and Dignity of the Human Being with regard to the Application of Biology and Medicine, both from 1997, and UNESCO's Universal Declaration on Bioethics and Human Rights, from 2005, place respect for human dignity as a central constraint on bioscience and biomedical practices (Beyleveld/Brownsword 2001, p. 29).

It will be argued below that utilizing human dignity as an absolute constraint on biotechnological interventions is not always consistent with the meaning of human dignity as a quality, a special status, or an intrinsic value that is shared by all human beings. The core themes in the concept of human dignity, in all its variations, reflect the respect for personhood or the human capacities that enable a human being to become a person, not necessarily the respect for every aspect of human nature as it is found in today's members of the species *Homo sapiens*.

A good example that demonstrates how human dignity can be construed as an absolute constraint on technological interventions that affect human nature is the case against the creation of experimental human chimaeras, which will be explored in the text.

2. Variations on Human Dignity

A common criticism among authors who discuss the meaning of human dignity and its application in bioethics is the vagueness with which dignity is employed in ethical, legal, and political discourses, often as a buzzword without a precise semantic definition.[1] Although this criticism holds true, dignity should not be simply brushed aside. Instead, a proper clarification of its meanings and ambiguities is necessary before attempting to give it a new signification.

Human dignity has a rich history in the Western philosophical tradition. It is not the goal of this chapter to discuss this history at length but only to note some common variations of the term that have influenced its current utilization as a means of preserving human nature.

Thus, according to the analysis of Nordenfelt (2010, pp. 69–81), there are mainly four different notions of dignity that permeate the current bioethical discourse, all of them somewhat relating to one another. Nordenfelt identifies (1) dignity as the intrinsic value of all humans (typically referred to by the German word *Menschenwürde*), (2) dignity as a quality that signifies individual merit, (3) dignity as the moral stature of an individual, and (4) dignity as identity or the respect that a human has for him/herself as a singular individual being with a history, a past, and a future and a specific set of relationships to others.

In all these notions, there are some common elements, as Nordenfelt (p. 70) indicates:

1. "Dignity" refers to a special dimension of value. In the case of *Menschenwürde* there is only one position on that scale, but with other kinds people can have different positions on the scale; they can be more or less dignified.
2. The dignity of a person is worthy of respect from others and from the person him or herself.
3. The dignity has a ground, normally a set of properties, belonging to the subject.

For the purposes of this text, it does not seem to be the case that the notion of human dignity being used as a defence of human nature relates specifically to individual excellence, a distinguished social status that some individuals may attain but others may not, or even the moral fortitude and self-respect some may achieve in contrast to the moral weakness of others. Indeed, if human dignity should prevent humans from changing their own natures, then it seems that "dignity", in this sense, relates much more to an intrinsic, special, and absolute value that all human beings equally have, that demands respect for "humanness", and that is grounded in properties that belong exclusively to humans.

Nevertheless, identifying a particular meaning of dignity as more relevant to this analysis does not imply that other meanings are irrelevant. There is significant interplay between the different meanings. Even if dignity is to be had, first and

1 Cf. Cochrane, 2010 and Macklin, 2003.

foremost, as an *unconditional* trait of humanity, then a *relational* sense of dignity may still be important in attempting to make sense of what exactly makes humans so special.

Some brief references to the historical meanings of dignity and the different forms that dignity has taken in the Western world are important in understanding the particular use of human dignity that is being analysed.

The Roman word *dignitas* was used to ascribe its bearer as noble or as the holder of a high office, based on an outstanding achievement that was recognized by others as worthy of honour and reverence (Chan 2015, p. 275). In this sense, someone could possess *dignitas* or not for reasons related to a particular individual's social standing.

Later, Christian theology came to regard human dignity as a God-given attribute of all men, due to their having been created in God's own image. In this sense, all humans shared a special status as beings created above all else in the universe.

A significant new development came with the Renaissance Italian humanist Giovanni Pico Della Mirandola (1463–1494), who, in his *Oration on the Dignity of Man* (pp. 4–5), wrote:

> Thou, constrained by no limits, in accordance with thine own free will, in whose hand We have placed thee, shalt ordain for thyself the limits of thy nature. [...] We have made thee neither of heaven nor of earth, neither mortal nor immortal, so that with freedom of choice and with honor, as though the maker and molder of thyself, thou mayest fashion thyself in whatever shape thou shalt prefer. Thou shalt have the power to degenerate into the lower forms of life, which are brutish. Thou shalt have the power, out of thy soul's judgement, to be reborn into the higher forms, which are divine.

Mirandola represents a significant milestone in the history of the idea of human dignity because he ascribes dignity to men due to their unique freedom of will and the power to shape themselves according to it. Humans are special – and hence uniquely dignified – because they can become whatever they want. His view represents a departure from the traditional Christian views up to that point in time because it announces a conception of dignity that attaches value not only to being created by God in His own image but also to the possibility of creating for oneself one's own unique destiny in life.

Subsequently, another important development in the history of human dignity was made by the German Enlightenment philosopher Immanuel Kant (1724–1804), who, in his *Groundwork of the Metaphysics of Morals* (pp. 52–53), wrote:

> In the realm of ends everything has either a *price* or a *dignity*. What has a price is such that something else can also be put in its place as its *equivalent*; by contrast, that which is elevated above all price, and admits of no equivalent, has a dignity. [...] Now morality

> is the condition under which alone a rational being can be an end in itself, because only through morality is it possible to be a legislative member in the realm of ends. Thus morality and humanity, insofar as it is capable of morality, is that alone which has dignity.

Kant equates dignity (or "worth") to the priceless capacity, intrinsic to humans, to act morally, to be an end in themselves and never a means to another's ends. Both Mirandola and Kant reach similar conclusions, albeit by different pathways: both believe that what makes human beings special and dignified is their unique ability to act freely. However, whereas Mirandola marvels at the unique versatility and indeterminate nature of human beings, Kant actually develops the idea that rational autonomy is the basis of human dignity, given that the only normative authority that can determine how to act morally (and, in the Kantian sense, freely) is reason.

Thus, if religious explanations are set aside, then the answer to the question concerning the grounds of the conception of human dignity as an intrinsic value of human beings seems to reside in the special human capacities that allow humans to act autonomously and to become whatever they wish to become.

Furthermore, a relational sense of dignity could derive from this if one considers the fact that although dignity is inherent, circumstances could drastically affect it. That is, all humans would possess intrinsic worth because they possess the capacities to act autonomously and to have freedom of will that allows them to make choices concerning their own lives. However, those capacities are socially developed and maintained. Without the actual means of developing and maintaining these capacities in a social setting, human dignity would remain an unfulfilled promise. Similarly, subjecting humans to treatment that reduces these capacities (for example, torture) would represent a degradation of human dignity.

Here, perhaps, the idea of basic human rights as duties of promotion of and respect for human dignity may come to the fore. Indeed, human dignity can be rightly regarded as the basis of human rights, in the sense that human rights are the rights that protect human beings, who deserve such special treatment simply because they share in a common humanity.

3. Human Dignity as a constraint to technological interventions?

Having provided a brief elaboration the conceivable secular meanings of human dignity as an intrinsic value in all human beings, it initially seems difficult to argue that this dignity could be a possible constraint on the use of technologies that should affect "human nature".

However, some commentators have noticed that the recent shift in which the idea of human dignity has been used neither as the basis of human rights nor as a call to respect personal autonomy (dignity as relational empowerment) but instead as "a duty not to compromise our own dignity as well as to act in a way that is compatible with respect for the vision of human dignity [of] a particular community" (Beyleveld/Brownsword, p. 1).

This shift apparently means that human dignity is threatened when some technologies are used to change aspects of human functioning that are deemed to be "sacred" or "essential" to specific views of what makes us human. In contrast to the view of dignity as relational empowerment, this view of dignity seems to be based on Western societies' lingering fear of the objectifying powers of modern science and how these powers may be employed in reductive attempts to explain and control humanity by engineering humans' genetic makeup, replacing body parts with machine components, or controlling reproductive processes.

Indeed, this communitarian view of human dignity can be employed as a reasonable deterrent against certain biotechnologies, for example, if a society, in a specific context, decides that human cloning for reproductive purposes should not be allowed because it somehow causes collective moral disgust in the community. Simultaneously, however, it would be relevant to analyse why something from which huge potential benefits could be reaped is regarded as morally disgusting.

On the other hand, human nature, by itself, does not seem to have a normative content. Human nature seems to be used in conjunction with human dignity as an imprecise word that conveys a vague sense of the distinguishing features that are shared by most humans in the current stage of evolution and that are not shared with other beings.

To observe the weakness of the claim of human dignity as a constraint to the use of certain technologies as a means of protecting human nature, let us turn to the example of the creation of human chimaeras by the introduction of genes from non-human animals (henceforth, animals) into the human germ line or even by fusing human and animal embryos. Technically, such experiments are very straightforward affairs (Savulescu 2003, pp. 22–25).

With regard to the purposes of such experiments, there are a few medical reasons to conduct them. Hybrid cells can be good source of embryonic stem cells for research, and creating chimerical cell lines may be useful for studying immunological features and aiding in finding cures for some diseases that affect the human immunological system. Additionally, combining human and animal genes may help create techniques to delay ageing, improve our current senses, or even give us new senses, which might be useful (Savulescu, pp. 22–23).

Would creating human-animal chimaeras offend human dignity? Certainly, it could be regarded as morally repugnant and disgusting, but why exactly?

Turning to the argument concerning human dignity, one could argue that blurring the boundaries of the human species threatens humanity's special place above all other creatures, that it alters the human genetic makeup for the sake of experiment, and that it undermines human identity and membership in the human family.[2]

However, these arguments express confusion between the biological concept of humanity and the moral and legal concept of personhood. The two concepts are often conflated, but they are not synonymous (Singer 2011, pp. 18–19). Being a person is an important part of what could be called "human nature" in Western societies. And it is so important that the concept of human dignity as relational empowerment exalts and protects exactly those human features that enable personhood to emerge, for example, self-consciousness, being able to act autonomously (according to practical reasons), and flourishing in social-communicative mediums.

Thus, it would seem that what genuinely constitutes the core of humanity, the essence that is worth protecting that has been referred to as dignified by numerous philosophers, is the human propensity to become persons, to act as moral agents, and to possess a sense of self-identity and self-purpose that is not determined by circumstance but rather emerges from it.

Following this line of reasoning, if the entire range of the more frequently occurring traits of the human species were taken into consideration, then not all of these traits would be worth protecting or preserving. Certainly, among those traits, there are some (perhaps many) that warrant protection, but others that do not. Human dignity should cover all of the features that are worth protecting but not all of them.

Paradoxically, then, it is likely that humans, in their attempts to protect, promote and enhance these human capacities, expand these capacities to super-human levels or that in the process, they lose other attributes that are also human or constitute their humanity but that are not, perhaps, worth preserving or protecting.

However, it could be argued that in a sense, becoming less human to enhance worthy and dignified human capacities is not particularly problematic. As observed above, certain capacities and abilities that allow for personhood have intrinsic value in human beings. In other words, in terms of technological interventions, human dignity should actually be used to defend against attacks against persons and personhood.

2 Cf. Robert, J. S./F. Baylis 2003.

Ultimately, human dignity should not be used indiscriminately as a constraint on the use and development of technologies that radically intervene in human nature. The normative force of dignity as a constraint in this case relates to assessing the danger that some of these technologies could be used to control human beings and make them more pliant and subservient, less autonomous, and less capable of devising their own destinies. In short, dignity entails a respect for persons and personhood and not necessarily a respect for humanity.

In this sense, there is not a genuine incompatibility between human dignity and transhumanism, for instance. In this discussion, this point is noteworthy because transhumanists are often accused of having disdain for human dignity exactly because they, indeed, have no awe and respect for human nature as a whole and are prone to tinkering with biotechnological possibilities to improve it.

Bostrom has already tackled this issue, but for the sake of emphasis, it bears repeating him. Bostrom argues that in any relevant sense of the word "dignity", posthumans would have at least as much of it as any human and, in some senses of the word, posthumans are likely to be much more dignified than humans (Bostrom 2005). Elaborating Bostrom's argument, human dignity is compatible with posthuman dignity because human dignity is not specific to humans but specific to persons; thus, any intervention that promotes personhood also promotes dignity.

5. Conclusions

Human dignity is a concept that can assume various meanings in different contexts. In the current legal and bioethical discourse, there seem to be two very diverse usages of the word that lead to distinct normative conclusions.

On one hand, in the tradition of both Mirandola and Kant, dignity may represent the inherent worth of beings who are capable of self-determination and moral choice. Expanding this notion further, it would not be enough to affirm dignity; dignity would have to be empirically and socially protected and promoted. Here, there is a sense of individual empowerment attached to human dignity, given that it seeks to enable human self-realization, with persons as ends in themselves. Dignity demands respect for personal autonomy and depends heavily on otherness as a condition for actualizing personhood. Thus, dignity is strongly relational, despite originating from atomist Kantian philosophy. Dignity as empowerment recognizes that what truly matters in humanity are the capacities that enable humans to become persons.

On the other hand, perhaps more in line with the tradition of Judaeo- Christian unconditional conceptions of human dignity, dignity may represent the absolute respect for a certain conception of humanness, which is based more on negative societal feelings of moral disgust and repugnance towards whatever can be regarded as affecting human nature. Here, dignity is attached to a belief that the human species holds a special high place against the backdrop of other biological species and that there are aspects of human nature that cannot be reduced to biological markers and technical artefacts.

The tension between both of these conceptions is irresolvable. The ethical-legal limits of what one is allowed to do with one's body and biology are bound to be set differently by societies, varying with several cultural, economic, social, and political vectors.

However, it must be noted that the tension is not between dignity and liberty or between dignity and autonomy. Indeed, as observed above dignity is strongly related to the status of human beings as free and self-determined beings. Additionally, prohibitions based on the second sense of human dignity noted above are intended to be provisional and subject to review according to the rules of democratic deliberation.

Furthermore, human dignity, as a normative principle, would be perfectly applicable to non-human entities – entities that may not qualify as *Homo sapiens*. A reappraisal of human moral attitudes towards their own supposed uniqueness would be necessary, but if an entity could have the capacity for autonomy, moral-practical judgements, and the pursuit of happiness, then there would not be a good reason to exclude it from the protective shroud of dignity.

Indeed, this view has some drawbacks. However, it seems that the advantages of shedding a view of human dignity as being tied to an immutable human nature outweigh them. It should be noted that the current knowledge on the field of genetics already blurs the boundaries between the human species and other biological species. In fact, human transgenesis has probably been a frequent occurrence (in evolutionary terms) (Fonseca/*et al.* 2012).

In short, human dignity, from an aesthetic perspective, has been tied to the almost metamorphic qualities of human persons. The multitude of ways in which humanity has expressed itself through the ages is ample proof of that. Fusions with machines and biological hybridism are merely the latest methods by which humans are attempting to remake themselves. These phenomena suggest that personhood offers better guidance to help draw the lines of new frontiers than humanness ever could.

References

Beyleveld, Deryck, Brownsword, Roger (2001): *Human Dignity in Bioethics and Biolaw*. OUP: Oxford.

Bostrom, Nick (2005): 'In Defense of Posthuman Dignity'. *Bioethics*. 19(3), pp. 202–214.

Chan, David K.: (2015) 'The Concept of Human Dignity In The Ethics of Genetic Research'. *Bioethics*. 29(4), pp. 274–282.

Cochrane, Alasdair (2010) 'Undignified Bioethics'. *Bioethics*. 24(5), pp. 234–241.

Fonseca, Flávio Guimarães da *et al.* (2012): 'Human Trangenesis: Definitions, Technical Possibilities and Moral Challenges'. *Philosophy & Technology*. 25(4), pp. 513–524.

Kant, Immanuel (2002): *Groundwork for the Metaphysics of Morals*. [Grundlegung zur Metaphysik der Sitten]. Yale University Press: New Haven.

Macklin, Ruth (2003): 'Dignity is a Useless Concept'. *British Medical Journal*. 327, 2003, pp. 1419–1420.

Mirandola, Giovanni Pico Della (1965): *Oration on The Dignity of Man*. [De hominis dignitate]. Bobbs-Merrill: Indianapolis.

More, Max (2013): 'The Philosophy of Transhumanism'. In: More, Max, Vita-More, Natasha Eds.: *The Transhumanist Reader: Classical and Contemporary Essays on the Science, Techonology, and Philosophy of the Human Nature*. Wiley-Blackwell: Oxford.

Nordenfelt, Lennart (2004): 'The Varieties of Dignity'. *Health Care Analysis*, 12(2).

Robert, J. S., F. Baylis (2013): 'Crossing species boundaries'. *The American Journal of Bioethics*. 3(3), 2003, pp. 69–81.

Sagoff, Mark (2005): 'Nature and Human Nature'" In: Baillie, Harold W., Casey, Timothy K. Eds.: *Is Human Nature Obsolete? Genetics, Bioengineering, and the Future of the Human Condition*. (Basic Bioethics). The MIT Press: Cambridge.

Savulescu, Julian (2003): 'Human-Animal Transgenesis and Chimeras Might Be an Expression of Our Humanity'. *American Journal of Bioethics*. 3(3), pp. 22–25.

Singer, Peter (2001): *Practical Ethics*. Cambridge University Press: Cambridge.

Schroeder, Doris (2012): 'Human Rights and Human Dignity – An Appeal to Separate the Conjoined Twins', *Ethical Theory Moral Practice*. 15, 2012, pp. 323–335.

Shultziner, Doron (2003): 'Human Dignity – Functions and Meanings'. *Global Jurist Topics*. 3(3), article 3.

Sulmasy, Daniel P. (2013) 'The Varieties of human dignity: a logical and conceptual analysis'. *Health Care and Philosophy*. 16, pp. 937–944.

Wojciech Załuski

The Concept of Person in the Light of Evolutionary Theory and Neuroscience

1. Introduction

The concept of person is permanently present in ethical discourse and plays in it an important role. In justification of this claim it suffices to recall that the thesis that human being is person underlies the categorical imperative in its formulation saying that human beings are never to be treated in an instrumental way, i.e., merely as a means, and not simultaneously as an end; or that the concept of person is also the central concept of one of the currents in normative ethics, viz. personalism, whose main ethical principle is *persona est affirmanda propter se ipsam*. However, the concept of person is not unproblematic. There are two main controversies around it. The first one concerns the question of *the very content of this concept* and a strictly related question of *when human being becomes a person*. This controversy has important implications for a number of particular bioethical problems, e.g., the admissibility of abortion, of *in vitro* insemination, of research on stem cells, or of biomedical cloning. However, we shall not deal with this controversy in our considerations; we shall focus on the second controversy. This controversy, of equal philosophical (though admittedly of lesser practical) importance as the first one, concerns the question of whether *human beings can at all be considered as persons*. The second controversy is not a philosophical problem that may or may not be highlighted by the achievements of the empirical sciences, but it is a problem *generated by these sciences*. The plan of our analysis is as follows. In section 2 we shall present two main conceptions of person: the ontological and the psychological. We shall argue that the conceptions are more similar than it might seem at the first sight, so that the question (analyzed in section 3) of whether the results of biological and neurocognitive sciences (the empirical sciences of direct relevance for philosophical-anthropological discussions) undermine the concept of person arises irrespective of which of the two conceptions is assumed.

2. Two conceptions of person

In the philosophical tradition two main conceptions of person were distinguished: the ontological (called also 'substantialist') and the psychological (called also 'asubstantialist'). The former assumes that every human being is a person on the basis of his/her human species membership only, whereas the latter assumes that only a being (human being or any other being) who is endowed with free will, fully rational, fully self-conscious is a person. It is worth noting that in the so-called 'classical' definition of person (formulated by Boethius), according to which *persona est individua substantia naturae rationalis*, both conceptions are in a sense present: the ontological, because this definition implies that a person is *substantia*, and the psychological, because it indicates rationality as a distinguishing feature of a person. Clearly, there are many different variants of both conceptions, but, given the goals of our analysis, we can discount this fact and content ourselves with the general accounts of these conceptions.

Prior to undertaking a more detailed analysis of both conceptions one clarifying remark may be in order. One may reasonably ask if the concept of person could not be dispensed with, given that it is (apparently) replaceable by the concept of 'human being' (if we assume the ontological conception of person) or the concept of 'a being who has free will, is fully rational and fully self-conscious' (if we assume the psychological conception). However, this doubt as to the usefulness of the concept of person can be easily removed. Such definitions would be inadequate substitutes of the concept of person because this concept *is not purely descriptive*; it has an additional evaluative component, viz. the in-built evaluative judgment that 'whatever *x* is a person, it has a special value – dignity – precisely by virtue of the fact that *x* is a person'. This component of the concept of person (thanks to which the concept is permanently present in ethical discourse as enabling the justification of various ethical principles) is lost in purely descriptive definitions thereof. Let us now return to the analysis of the two conceptions.

The two conceptions, though *prime facie* quite distinct, are in fact closely connected. The connection becomes apparent when as ask the adherent of the ontological conception, why human being should be regarded as a being endowed with a special value (dignity), i.e. as a person. He can answer this question in two different ways, trying to ground this concept either theologically or non-theologically. In the former case he shall say that human being is a being distinguished by God (created in His own image and likeness), and this fact confers dignity upon the whole mankind. In the latter case he shall say that each human being is at least *potentially* a being who has free will, is fully rational and fully self-conscious, and this fact confers dignity upon the whole mankind.

As we can see, the connection exists between the ontological conception of person grounded theologically and the psychological conception of person: both conceptions assume in fact identical criteria of personhood. The difference between them stems from the fact that the former allows their potential realization, and the latter requires their actual realization. Of course, the difference is, from the practical standpoint, not negligible, since it may lead to different practical consequences in the context of bioethical controversies: given that each person in the psychological sense is a person in the ontological sense, but not *vice versa*, the adherents of the psychological conception will refuse to recognize dignity of human beings who do not actually fulfill the three criteria of personhood (e.g., human beings who are mentally ill, in a vegetative state, with advanced Alzheimer illness, or fetuses); these human beings are regarded by the adherents of the ontological conception, by virtue of the human species membership, as equally valuable (endowed with dignity) as other human beings. But the difference is negligible given the goals of our analysis, viz. reflection on whether the results of the empirical sciences undermine the concept of person. Let us summarize:

Conceptions of person:

(1) Ontological

  (a) grounded theologically
  (b) grounded non-theologically

(2) Psychological

Ways of applying the results of biological and neurocognitive sciences in discussions about the concept of person:

(1) In order to determine the point at which human being becomes a person.
(2) In order to analyze whether human beings fulfill the criteria of personhood (the conceptions of person potentially 'endangered' by the results of the aforementioned sciences are the ontological conception grounded non-theologically and the psychological conception).

It should be added that these two ways, which we distinguished according to two main controversies around the concept of persons, are not the only ones. One may also argue that the biological and neurcognitive sciences enable one to demonstrate that our thinking in terms of 'persons' is natural, i.e., in-built in our genotype as a result of our evolutionary history. Such an argumentation would be a *sui generis* attempt at naturalizing Peter Strawson's claim (developed in his *Individuals*) that predicates referring to persons (the so-called 'P predicates') constitute a necessary element of our conceptual scheme. This kind of (fairly plausible) argumentation was developed, e.g., by Martha J. Farah and Andrea S. Heberlein (cf. Farah, Heberlien, pp. 37–38). These authors, however, also argue for an implausible claim that the very fact that our thinking in terms of persons is an evolutionary product, undermines the concept of person, since it (purportedly) implies that this concept is illusionary, deprived of any real correlate. This way of appealing to the results of the empirical sciences with a view to undermining the concept of persons, seems to us misguided: from the fact that a given category *x* of thinking is an evolutionary product, one cannot infer that *x* does not refer to anything real, that it plays only a practical role of efficiently guiding our behavior, and thereby facilitating achieving our evolutionary goals. One must provide additional arguments for such a bold claim (that *x* – an evolutionary product – has no real correlate), and no such arguments are provided by Farah and Heberlein. A much more natural way of appealing to the results of science with a view to undermining the concept of person, seems to us the way (2), which consists in investigating whether the results of the sciences allow us to maintain that human beings posses the traditional attributes of the person. We shall develop this way in the next section. As we shall see, this way may inspire an attempt at constructing a *third* conception of person, different both from the ontological and the psychological.

3. The attributes of persons and the results of biological and neurocognitive sciences

As mentioned above, the traditional attributes of person – the criteria of personhood – are free will, full rationality, and full self-consciousness. Now, one can argue that the results of the biological and neurocognitive sciences show that the three criteria are never fulfilled or fulfilled only to a degree, and that thereby these results undermine the concept of person. Let us present and assess this argumentation in more detail.

(*Free will*) An agent *A* has free will if he/she, for any time t_i, had at time t_i the ability to make a different decision from the one he/she actually made at time t_i. This ability is usually called 'the ability to do otherwise'. The thesis that the agent *A* has free will implies therefore that at time t_i, at which he/she made a given decision, he/she could have made a different decision. It means that at time t_i all options considered by the agent were, so to speak, *authentic*, i.e., the past did not determine the decision that was actually made. Freedom of will is therefore an agent's capacity by virtue of which his/her decisions are not elements of causal chains but are initiated by the agent in an absolute or quasi-absolute manner. The thesis about the existence of free will implies then a non-reductionist, dualistic view of the human mind (the human mind, as distinct from the brain, being the *locus* of free will). Let us now see what implications for the problem of the existence of free will may have the results of the biological and neurocognitive sciences. *Firstly*, one may argue that the results provide a strong case for the reductionist, materialist-monistic view of the human mind: a standard philosophical interpretation of the correlations (ascertained in many experiments and observed in the context of various brain lesions) between the changes in the brain and the changes in the mind is that the mind is reducible to the brain. And since the brain is a deterministic mechanism[1], human decisions can be explained (or, rather, could be explained at some more advanced stage of the science's development) in a deterministic way as a result of the causal interactions at the neuronal level. Thus, so the argument goes, in the light of the achievements of the biological and neurocogntive sciences our mental states (e.g., intentions or deliberations) do not possess a causal force: they are epiphenomena of the brain states, and people mistakenly believe them to influence our decisions. If this view is correct, then reason-based explanations of human decisions are wrong, or at least non-fundamental: the proper explanations of human decisions are the causal ones, tracing the chains of neuronal interactions issuing in given decisions.

Secondly, one may argue that Benjamin Libet's famous experiments provide a scientific argument against the existence of free will. As is well known, these experiments show that brain activity, i.e., the activity of the so-called readiness potential registered when an agent prepares for an action, precedes by a few hundred milliseconds the agent's conscious decision to take this action (cf., e.g., Libet 2005; Wegner 2002). These experiments are often interpreted as providing a support for the epiphenomenal account of the relations between the brain and the mind, according to which it is our brain that 'makes' the decisions, which are later 'reflected' at the level of consciousness.

However, it must be emphasized that none of the above two ways of criticizing the thesis about the existence of free will is conclusive and unobjectionable. As for the first one, the results of biological and neurocognitive sciences can perhaps rightly be regarded as better harmonizing with the reductionist, materialist-monist view of the mind than with the non-reductionist, dualist view. But it does not mean that these results cannot be reconciled with the latter view: there are a number of philosophers who provide serious arguments not only for the possibility of the reconciliation of the dualist view of the human mind with the results of the biological and neurocognitive sciences, but also for the stronger claim

---

1 We discount the question of the possible influence of non-deterministic events – from the quantum level – on our decisions, because we agree with the view that decisions caused by events from the quantum level would not be free in the sense in which the concept of free decision is understood by the adherents of the thesis about the existence of free will.

that certain phenomena from the level of consciousness (deliberation, rationality, self-control) cannot be explained within the materialist-monist view of the mind (cf., e.g., Popper, Eccles 2001; Swinburne 2013; Hasker 1999; Stapp 2004; Schwartz, Begley 2002). As for the second one, Libet's experiments can be criticized on various grounds, of which we shall point at the following two: (1) these experiments concern very simple decisional situations, and it is not clear whether the findings made in their context can be extrapolated to 'real-life', complex decisional situations; (2) each case of 'compatibility' between the brain's decision and the conscious decision can be interpreted as attesting the fact that the mind *accepted* the brain's decision but just as well could *veto* it if it willed so (interestingly, this interpretation was accepted by Benjamin Libet).

To conclude, it is by no means clear whether the results of biological and neurocognitive sciences undermine the thesis about the existence of free will: one cannot exclude the possibility that the standard (reductionist, materialist-monist) philosophical interpretation of the correlations between the changes in the brain and the changes in the mind may seem 'natural' but is in fact wrong, and in retrospect (as the science goes forward) its dominance in the present 'climate of opinion' will be viewed as a product of *naïve and superficial thinking.*

(*Full rationality*) The concept of full rationality can be defined in the following way: *an agent is fully rational if and only if he/she (a) maximizes her utility function, (b) does not discount her future utility hyperbolically, (c) does not discount her future utility too heavily and thereby attaches sufficient importance to future utility.*[2] The condition (b) needs some further explanation[3]. An agent discounts the utility of a future reward hyperbolically if she discounts it in inverse proportion to the reward's expected delay: the more delayed the reward is, the less discounted it is.[4] This means that the discounted value of a future reward initially rises very slowly, but it starts soaring rapidly when the moment of receiving it approaches. Thus, a characteristic feature of hyperbolic discounting is that it is not stationary, i.e., that

2 The condition (c) can be put almost equivalently in many different, less technical ways. One can say that an agent should have a long time horizon; be patient; not be myopic; be capable of deferring gratification, i.e., of choosing a greater good offering a more distant satisfaction rather than a lesser good offering immediate satisfaction; be not impulsive; not prefer a smaller good now over a disproportionately larger good later.

3 The fragment that follows is based on my book *Evolutionary Theory and Legal Philosophy* (Zaluski 2009, pp. 9–10).

4 The phenomenon of hyperbolic discounting was discovered by Richard J. Herrnstein in experiments involving pigeons and food and further analyzed by various researchers, e.g., by George Ainslie (cf. Ainslie 2001).

its dynamic does not remain the same at all time points. This kind of discounting is called 'hyperbolic', because a discount function corresponding to it has the hyperbola-like shape – it is deeply bowed and steeply rising. A simple example of such a function is $U(x \text{ at } t_j) = U(x \text{ at } t_k)/(1 + rt)$. This function expresses the fact that the utility of some reward x at time t_k (the time it becomes available) is discounted by an agent to the value at time t_j (which is t units of time into the past from t_k) by a discount factor $1/(1 + rt)$, where $r \geq 0$ is a discount rate characteristic for the agent (r can be called 'the measure of the agent's impatience'). Let us now see to what consequences this kind of discounting leads in a situation in which an agent has to choose between a smaller reward available at an earlier time t_1 and a larger reward available at a later time t_2 (it is assumed that the agent cannot have both rewards simultaneously). This situation is depicted by the following figure:

Fig. 1: Hyperbolic discounting.

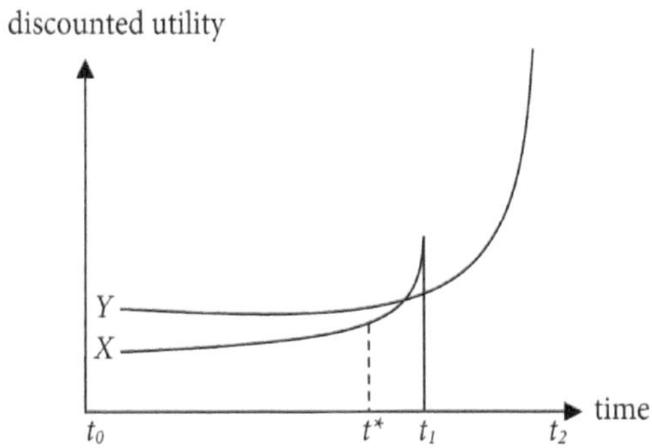

Y and X are the agent's present value curves of, respectively, the larger, later reward (available at t_2), and the smaller, sooner reward (available at t_1). In the time interval $[t_0, t^*)$ the agent prefers to choose the larger, later reward rather than the smaller, sooner reward. However, at time t^* (the agent's point of indifference between the rewards) a reversal of her preferences takes place (which is illustrated in Figure 1 by the crossing of the curves). In consequence, in the time interval $(t^*, t_1]$ the present value of the smaller reward exceeds that of the larger reward. Now, unless the agent takes some precautionary measures, she will yield to the temptation to choose the smaller reward at t_1 for which she has a temporary preference, thereby depriving herself of the opportunity to receive the larger reward at t_2. This effect – called 'the temptation effect' – is the direct consequence of the fact that the dynamics of hyperbolic discounting increases rapidly as the moment of the receiving of the reward comes.[5] Thus, in situations in which an agent who discounts the future hyperbolically has to choose between a smaller, sooner reward and a larger, later reward her behaviour will not only be time-inconsistent (which is itself sufficient to call it 'irrational') but will also cause her to sustain utility loss, because she will succumb to the temptation to choose the smaller one as soon as it becomes available.

Now, as is well known, numerous experiments show that agents systematically violate the conditions of full rationality. *Firstly, people violate axioms that have to be satisfied by their preferences if these preferences are to be expressible by utility functions* (if an agent's preferences do not satisfy these axioms, they cannot be expressed by a utility function, and consequently there is nothing to be maximized). For instance, their preferences often violate the axioms of completeness (given options *A* and *B*, people do not exactly know which one they prefer) and transitivity (given options *A*, *B*, *C*, people prefer *A* to *B*, *B* to *C*, and *C* to *A*). Many other instances of the violations of these axioms have been observed, e.g., the so-called framing effect, which consists in that people derive different conclusions from the same data if these data are presented to them in different ways, e.g., an agent is more likely to accept a given solution if we say to her that this solution will make 60 (out of 100) people survive than if we say to her that it will make 40 (out of 100) people die.

Secondly, people have serious problems assessing objective probabilities of states of affairs, e.g., instead of carefully analyzing all the facts necessary for this assessment, they use mental short-cuts – 'heuristics', which often lead to erroneous results. Let us mention here one of the best-known heuristics – the availability heuristic, discovered and described by Daniel Kahneman and Amos Tversky. This

5 Let us present a few examples illustrating hyperbolic discounting. (1) Ann is to choose between the 'smaller, sooner reward' Xavier – a less attractive candidate for her husband who declares at *t0* that he will marry her in one year (t_1) – and the 'larger, later reward' Yves – a more attractive candidate for her husband who declares at *t0* that he will marry her only in two years (t_2). At *t0* Ann prefers to marry Yves. However, since Ann discounts her future rewards hyperbolically, the present value of the sooner candidate will rise rapidly at time t^* (say, after 10 months from t_0), so that a reversal of her preferences will take place, and she will yield to the temptation to marry Xavier at t_1. (2) An agent prefers $15 ten days from now to $10 nine days from now, and at the same time she prefers $10 today to $15 tomorrow even though it is the same choice seen at ten days' distance. (3) An agent prefers a glass of exquisite wine in four hours to a glass of poor wine in two hours and at the same time she prefers a glass of poor wine right now to a glass of exquisite wine in two hours, even though it is the same choice seen at two hours' distance.

heuristic consists in people ascribe higher probability to the type of events whose instances they can bring to mind more easily. This heuristic often leads to correct results because the probability of events that can be easily recalled is often indeed higher. But, obviously, this method of assessing probabilities may prove to be misleading, for the simple reason that some events are more easily recalled not because they are frequent but because they exert a strong influence on our imagination.[6]

Thirdly, many experiments show that agents discount their future welfare hyperbolically; as Ainslie (2001, p. 35) wrote: "it [discount curve – W.Z] is clearly hyperbolic for all age groups, although older subjects discount the future less steeply than younger ones, introverts less steeply than extroverts, and ordinary adults less steeply than heroin addicts or even smokers." Likewise, many experiments show that people often deploy irrationally high discount rates. All the above facts provide a strong support for the claim that human being are not fully rational, but only imperfectly rational.

(*Full self-consciousness*) The results of biological and neurocognitive sciences undermine the 'Cartesian' thesis that human beings manifest full self-consciousness, i.e., they know, or at least they can know if they want, all their mental states, thereby being (or being able to be) fully transparent to themselves. *Firstly*, the results of these sciences show that the overwhelming part of the activities of the human mind have an automatic and unconscious character. This fact is fully understandable, given that automatization of our mental activities is the most effective solution (the conscious activities are very energy-consuming), and thereby has been 'preserved' by natural selection (cf., e.g., Wilson 2002). There is yet another evolutionary argument for the claim that most of our mental activities should be expected to have an unconscious character: our brain was gradually shaped in the process of evolution, by introducing subsequent 'parts' to it; and since, to our best knowledge, most, if not all, mental processes of our animal ancestors, with which we share large parts of the brain, have an unconscious character, then it is by no means surprising that the overwhelming majority of the activities of our mind have an unconscious character.

6 Compare the following quotation: "(t)he impact of seeing a house burning on our estimate of probability of such accidents is greater than the impact of reading about a fire in the local paper. Furthermore, recent occurrences are likely to be more available than earlier occurrences: it is a common experience that our estimate of probability of traffic accidents rises temporarily when one sees a car overturned by the side of the road." (Tversky, Kahneman 1974, p. 1128).

Secondly, the human mind is not designed to seek for the truth as end in itself but to seek the truth only in so far as it helps to solve the adaptive problems. The human mind is therefore essentially practical: it copes well above all with practical problems connected with survival and reproduction that our ancestors encountered in the evolutionary past. Given that the human mind is not a disinterested truth-seeker, one can expect that it will be prone to generate various illusions, if this is the best way for solving a concrete adaptive problem. For instance, a well-established fact is that humans are prone to self-deception, i.e., to unconscious concealing information from themselves and thereby to distorting their picture of reality. As Michele K. Surbey (2004, p. 140) put it:

> "The self-deceptive mechanisms have potentially arisen as the outcome of a number of selective forces: natural selection for cognitive efficiency, maintenance of a positive outlook and hope in adversity, concealment of threatening thoughts that could limit adaptive responding, the ability to form mutually beneficial social alliances; kin selection for smooth family relationships; and sexual selection for success in mate selection and retention. … At moderate levels, self-deception promotes mental health and effective coping with environmental demands. At extremely low or high levels, individual or collective self-deception may have detrimental consequences."

Thirdly, our memory, on which our self-consciousness and personal identity is based, is very fallible. For instance, we remember only a small part of the events we experienced, and even this small part is remembered in a very imperfect way (cf. Schacter 2002).

4. Conclusions

The foregoing considerations were aimed at showing how the results of the biological and neurocognitive sciences can be invoked in the argumentation for the thesis the human beings do not fulfil the criteria of personhood, and thereby that they are not persons (either in the ontological, non-theologically grounded sense or in the psychological sense, since, as was argued, both conceptions assume in fact the same criteria of personhood).

However, it seems that *the claim that the biological and neurocognitive sciences undermine the concept of person would be precocious.* The only criteria of personhood that they indeed undermine are full rationality and full self-consciousness. It is by no means obvious whether they undermine the thesis about the existence of free will, which, one may argue, is the *principal* criterion of personhood (accordingly, it would not be the case that each of the three criteria is a necessary condition and their conjunction a sufficient condition of ascribing the status of person to a human being; rather, the necessary and sufficient condition of personhood would be free will, the remaining ones would be *subsidiary*, thus making personhood a *gradable* status).

Furthermore, one may plausibly maintain that the belief in the existence of free will is a metaphysical belief that cannot be falsified by appealing to the results of the empirical sciences. And since this belief is strictly connected with the belief in the aptness of the non-reductionist, dualist view of the human mind, this view of the human mind cannot be falsified by the results of the empirical sciences either.

Thus, precisely speaking, *if we agree that free will is the most important criterion of personhood, the results of the empirical sciences will never necessitate the rejection of the concept of person*. But let us assume, counterfactually, that the belief in the existence of free will has been falsified. Would it mean that we have to reject the claim that human beings are persons? Clearly so, if the only conceptions of the person were the two analyzed above. But it may be possible to construct a different conception of person, based on *weaker* criteria. These criteria would no longer be freedom of will, full rationality, and full self-consciousness, but freedom from coercion (reconcilable with the deterministic account of human decisions and with the materialist-monist view of the human mind), limited rationality, and limited self-consciousness.

The analysis of the problem of whether these criteria are indeed sufficient for conferring upon human beings the status of persons (and thereby for endowing them with a special value – dignity, and justifying treating them as moral agents responsible for their actions) lies beyond the scope of this paper. However, it is worth noticing that many philosophers belonging to the empiricist tradition (e.g. David Hume) undertook efforts to base the concept of moral agency on such – weaker – criteria (e.g., on the criterion of freedom of coercion rather than freedom of will). It remains the hardly contested fact, though, that the best justification for treating human as persons is provided not by those weaker criteria, but by the strong ones – free will, full rationality, and full self-consciousness (and especially by the first of the three).

References

Ainslie, George (2001): *Breakdown of Will*. Cambridge University Press, Cambridge.

Farah, Martha J., Heberlein, Andrea S. (2007): 'Personhood and Neuroscience: Naturalizing or Nihilating'. *American Journal of Bioethics – Neuroscience*, 7 (1), pp. 37–48.

Hasker, William (1999): *The Emergent Self*. Cornell University Press: Ithaca, London.

Libet, Benjamin (2005): *Mind Time. The Temporal Factor in Consciousness.* Harvard University Press: Cambridge, Massachusetts, London, England.

Popper, Karl R., Eccles, John C. (2006): *The Self and its Brain. An Argument for Interactionism.* Routledge: London and New York.

Schwartz, Jeffrey, Begley, Sharon (2002): *The Mind and the Brain: Neuroplasticity and the Power of Mental Force.* ReganBooks: New York.

Searle, John (2001): *Rationality in Action.* The MIT Press: Cambridge, Mass., London, England.

Stapp, Henry (2004): *Mind, Matter and Quantum Mechanics.* Springer: Berlin, Heidelberg.

Surbey, Michele. K. (2004): 'Self-Deception: Helping and Hindering Personal and Public Decision Making'. In: Crawford, Charles/ Salmon, Catherine Eds.: *Evolutionary Psychology, Public Policy and Personal Decisions*, Lawrence Erlbaum Associates: Mahwah.

Swinburne, Richard (2013): *Mind, Brain, and Free Will.* Oxford University Press: Oxford.

Tversky, Amos, Kahneman, Daniel (1974): 'Judgment under Uncertainty: Heuristics and Biases'. *Science*, 185, pp. 1124–1131.

Wegner, Daniel M. (2002): *The Illusion of Conscious Will.* MIT Press: Cambridge, Massachusetts, London, England.

Wilson, Timothy. D. (2002): *Strangers to Ourselves. Discovering the Adaptive Unconscious.* The MIT Press: Cambridge, Massachusetts, London, England.

Załuski, Wojciech (2009): *Evolutionary Theory and Legal Philosophy.* Edward Elgar: Cheltenham, UK.

Carolina Nasser, Nara Carvalho, Brunello Stancioli and Laís Lopes

An Adequate Concept of Human Body: Debunking Mind-Body Dualism

1. Introduction

Mental processes are key to virtually everything that is important in Law. In examples such as rom states of raw emotions, deep rationality, autonomy and decision-making, behaviours and *selves* are constructed along with mental processes.

Traditionally, mental processes and bodily states are individually analysed. Boundaries between bodily phenomena and mental phenomena are often perceived as being sharp and clearly distinctive. Mental processes are usually associated with pure rationality and bodies are regarded as receptacles of advanced mental cognition. In short, this is the notion of mind-body dualism.

This essay brings together Law, Philosophy of Mind and contemporary Neuroscience, to debunk mind-body dualism because this dualism leads legal approaches to mystifying personhood and legal subjects. Therefore, the following sections will be empirically oriented to offer an alternative view of the mind-body problem, which is strongly connected to contemporary studies on minds, bodies and environments.

2. An Overview on the mind-body problem and a possible way out

The relationship between mind and body has been a target of investigation in many diverse niches of Western Philosophy. Inquiries regarding the exact complexity and attributes of the possible connection between these entities are often treated as one philosophical problem, which contains an array of other scientific and practical problems.

Yearning for clarification on this subject is at the centre of the so-called *mind-body problem*. The distinctive features of the problem are typically bisected into practical inquiries. To begin, analyses are aimed at the character, or nature, of a *mind* and of a *body* and whether both are distinct or the same entity.

Not since René Descartes have the controversies around the search for accurate answers to the mind-body problem been so frequently discussed in Western Philosophy, both Continental and Analytic. Purely incidentally, the problem has been examined at this scope. According to M. Stone, "it is significant that these modern and contemporary problems [those connected to the mind-body problem] were not recognised as such by successive generations of medieval thinkers." (Stone 2002, p. 34)

Scholastic and religious thought was a great influence on the majority of medieval thinkers. It was presumed that the so-called unitary nature of human beings gave credence to the queries about minds, bodies and souls. Created through an image of a God, human beings were thought be integrated by both immaterial and material components. This integration was addressed so superficially that Stone said, "Medieval discussions of the soul were of an entirely different type and order from modern debates about the mind." (Stone 2002, p. 35)[1].

That the Cartesian tradition is considered the starting point of the mind-body problem – as it is portrayed today – appears indisputable among philosophers of the mind[2]. Nevertheless, some space must be dedicated to the discussion of Descartes' writings to distinguish between the features of the French philosopher's works and the post-Cartesian substantial dualism tradition.

2.1 Descartes' view on minds and bodies

In *Discourse on the method*, Descartes looks for a metaphysical foundation above doubts. Therefore, he rejects a vast amount of previously obtained knowledge by never admitting anything as rightful without doubts. According to Descartes, it is important to never "accept anything for true which [he] did not clearly know to be such" (Descartes, René: *Discourse on method of rightly conducting one's reason and of seeking truth in the sciences* [Kindle Edition]. Retrieved from Amazon, p. 21).

Through this procedure, Descartes discovered what he considered to be a solid and definite truth, an unswerving fact even for sceptics: *cogito ergo sum*, or the first principle of his philosophy – the modern subject, the modern self. Such a thinking substance distinct from other corporeal substrata could, then, stem only from a divine rationality.

---

1 We note that Thomas Aquinas discussed rudiments of the mind-body relation under a strong Aristotelian tradition. According to Aquinas, a human being is a unity. A self creates all actions that come from bodies – except thoughts and desires, both being immaterial and intellectual. Intellectual activities promote what Aquinas calls a "two world encounter": the spiritual and the material worlds. It is not in the scope of the present article, however, to discuss this approach to the mind-body problem. For further information on Aquinas' view on minds and bodies: Stone 2002, pp. 34–69.

2 Such as Neil Levy, Kirk Ludwig, David Chalmers, and Sarah Patterson, among many others.

Descartes then formulated his *Meditations on first philosophy* to, among other purposes, make explicit his understanding of the *cogito* as a truth. In this work, "[t]he substance of the argument is very similar: but its ordering is altered, in ways that are philosophically significant." (Moriarty 2008, p. xiii)

As suggested in the very title of the *Meditations*, Descartes sought to demonstrate and clarify both the alleged fact of one God's existence – a subject that we will not discuss in the current paper – and the distinction between body and soul[3] in human beings. The *Meditations* are organised into three sections. For the scope of this text, we shall focus on the second.

In his second meditation, he begins to draw his first certainty. In this passage, it is possible to catch sight of the rudiments of a Cartesian concept of mind. This notion is developed through the struggle that Descartes identifies between sceptical views about epistemology and the search for the nature of the human soul and of a God. According to Sarah Patterson, this struggle "results in a retreat to a subjective realm of thought and experience which is both better known than the external world of bodies and metaphysically distinct from it." (Patterson 2002, p. 76)

To Descartes, human beings were thinking things, and through his *cogito*, he reversed the very rationale of scepticism. The primordial functions of a living rational being could be located in the soul (mind) and diffused throughout the body. The faculty of rational thought is inseparable from the *cogito*. In this sense, bodies and souls would not be form and matter but two unreservedly different substances.

Still, the importance of the possession of a soul for Descartes' thought is ground-breaking and influences an entire tradition in Western Philosophy regarding dualism between bodies and minds and between humans and animals, because human minds cannot be made from matter. To the French thinker, "rather than being alive by virtue of possessing souls, the life of animals consists in the fact that their bodily parts move in certain ways." (James 2002, p. 122)

The legacy of Descartes' way of thinking influences several niches of knowledge. With respect to philosophy of mind and the mind-body problem, his bequest has generated the *dualist hypothesis on the mind-body problem*. This *iconic* Descartes, as Susan James asserts, usually emphasises to the sharp and strict division between matter and mind – a material body and an immaterial soul (James 2002, p. 111).

3 Descartes does not stress terminological differences among soul, self or mind.

2.2 Dualism and internalism on the mind-body problem: a Descartes' legacy

Dualism generally consists of the division of some concept into two opposing, or contrasting aspects[4]. In the specific case of the mind-body problem, dualism corresponds to the view that mind and body possess different characteristics, or natures, and are substantially dissociated. They neither share the same nature nor come from the same origin. The analysis of dualism that we will conduct in this paper is centred on substantial dualism or ontological anti-reductionism[5].

There is a great quantity of precepts concerning the mind-body problem, which contain some sort of ideological bias, as Mario Bunge clarifies (Bunge 1977, p. 501). Dualism is probably one of the most dramatic examples of that partiality because it provides philosophical support to religious theories of the immortality of the soul and a subsequent reward in an after-death[6]. Moreover, according to Neil Levy,

> [i]f the soul is immaterial, then there is no reason to believe that it is damaged by the death and decay of the body; the soul is free, after death, to re-join God and the heavenly hosts (themselves composed of nothing but soul-stuff). (Levy 2007, p. 9)

2.2.1 *Substantial mind-body dualism*

Cartesian substantial dualism states that mind and matter are different substances. The rational subject, or the human being for Cartesian thought, surpasses the physical universe because pure matter is not endowed with rational behaviour or thought. Thus, matter and mind are fenced off.

Pure matter corresponds to the physical world, whereas immaterial substance represents the mind, whose main property is to give rise to thoughts. Influenced by mechanicism in philosophical thought, Cartesian thought states on the one hand that the physical world is mechanized. On the other hand, rational minds cannot possess this mechanization. Animals, for example, might even display complex behaviour, although they do not possess any sort of mind.

---

4 The Oxford Dictionary.

5 We are aware that "bundle dualism" is also important for the development of the dualist approach to the mind-body problems. Nonetheless, for our current scope, we will focus on the dualism that stems from René Descartes and not from thinkers such as David Hume. We also know that several authors, such as Derek Parfit, characterize their theories of minds and bodies as "bundle theory", although their horizon is eminently materialistic. For further views on ontological anti-reductionism, see Ludwig, 2003, p. 13.

6 These beliefs are widespread in Western cultural heritage.

Only incidentally is the interaction between minds and material environments considered by Cartesian dualism. The rational nature of minds, therefore, does not arise from any sort of interaction between them. Although minds can display interactive patterns, the contents of their rationality are not unfolded through interaction but stem from the essential property of minds, namely, to think. Thereby, mental phenomena and corporeal phenomena cannot be analysed as forms and matters but as two substances of entirely different natures.

2.3 Debunking the Cartesian mind-body dualism

The meaning of minds and bodies according to Cartesian dualism can be summarised, roughly, in this way: minds and bodies are different and independent substances, which are parallel and come into some sort of contact but do not define themselves together through interaction.

Throughout the 20th and 21st centuries, however, branches such as linguistics, neuroscience and informational technologies have changed how the mind-body problem is analysed. They have garnered data suggesting that a dualist response to the problem is scientifically infeasible. The hypothesis that minds and bodies are two different substances, one of them immaterial, is scientifically implausible. It has been shown, instead, that minds and bodies are at least materially intertwined – if they differ at all.

2.3.1 Matter matters: the case of Phineas Gage

Interdependence between mental and physical events can be observed through the direct influence of corporeal events on mental-based behaviour, such as sense of past, present and future and coherence of a self throughout time. The case of Phineas Gage, broadly discussed among mind-body problem authors, is an example of this contingency[7].

Gage was a disciplined, hardworking employee of a railroad line in the United States. While at work, Gage suffered a serious injury: a tamping iron went through his skull after an explosion, leaving him with a skull fracture and massive brain damage. The most affected area was the ventromedial prefrontal cortex (vmPFC). Gage underwent risky surgery and survived. His behaviour, however, changed radically. Gage became aggressive and reckless, unable to carry out long-term plans.

7 One of the most specific discussion of the Phineas Gage case was developed by Antonio Damasio, *cf.* Damasio, 1994, pp. 3–79.

Although brains do not have areas dedicated to a single behavioural function, some areas are more specialized than others. In other words, brain areas are distinguishable, not disentangled. For example, the vmPFC is closely linked to social decision-making[8]. Still, these areas interact directly with other structures of the human body to produce "rational" patterns of action.

Since Gage, the vmPFC has been subjected to countless studies. Neurological investigation has suggested that vmPFC damage affects not only "*directly* upon rationality, but upon the relationship between the brain and the rest of the body." (Bechara 1998, p. 428–429)

Antoine Bechara *et al.* have shown (1998) that lesions in the vmPFC prevent the human body from receiving warning signs through skin conductance responses (SCRs). Human beings who produce anticipation SCRs usually have greater inclination to avoid risky behaviour. Thus, people with vmPFC damage rely solely on brain anticipations – therefore without the benefits of a brain-body-based cognition.

The disadvantage caused by the lack of SCR warnings leads injured people to make less rational strategic decisions. They are, therefore, more reckless than those without brain damage. The results highlight that "VM lesion patients are oblivious to the future and are guided predominantly by immediate prospects. This 'myopia for the future' persists in the face of increasing adverse consequences." (Bechara/Tranel/Damasio 2000, p. 2198)

The notion that not only the brain but also the entire body is responsible for decision-making is central to António Damasio's theory of the centrality of bodily events in decision-making. Cognition is, in this sense, incomplete without the action of bodily events on decision-making rationality. According to Neil Levy, if the mind is to be understood as something rational, "(…) then the mind includes (parts of) the body, at least for some purposes and in some contexts." (Levy 2007, p. 32)

2.3.2 Language

Another key aspect of the interdependence between mental and physical events can be analysed through the scope of language making and reading processes.

It is known that the process of making language and the mastering of reading/writing are important types of adroitness in the development of the human species and human societies. It has recently been suggested that they are not innate

8 xxx.

skills – as anthropology, linguistics and biological sciences used to suggest – but true evolutionary acquisitions. As Maryanne Wolf indicates,

> [W]e were never born to read. Human beings invented reading only a few thousand years ago. And with this invention, we rearranged the very organization of our brain, which in turn expanded the ways we were able to think, which altered the intellectual evolution of our species. (Wolf 2008, p. 3)

Acquisition of reading skills and mastering of language change the human organism as a whole, resulting in changes in behaviour and decision-making processes. These effects are possible only because of the plasticity of the human brain, once the recruitment of neurons is affected by every new skill acquired. Neuronal plasticity means that behaviours and decisions regarding mental processes do not involve non-communicative and segregated neurons, as was once believed. Instead, they involve neuronal structures as a whole, which are adaptive and incorporative.

In this sense, it is possible to acquire some skill, such as reading, only if a complex system, such as the human body, is plastic enough to be rearranged to produce this skill – in a two-way interaction. Still, complexity and language organization directly affect the very bodily structures of human bodies. In this regard, the brain structures of, for example, Mandarin readers differ significantly from those of an English reader. Thus, when Chinese read in English for the first time, they tend to recruit the specific reading structures of Mandarin, once "[t]he act of learning Chinese characters has literally shaped the Chinese reading brain."(Wolf 2008, p. 5)

Hence, acquisition of complex abilities or skills, such as language, demands an active engagement with informational environments – a process that cannot be regarded as innate or given. Language enables human beings (and in fact other animals that have developed this skill) to organize thoughts in a way that would be unimaginable without the domain of language.

At an elementary level, therefore, mind-body dualism is flawed. Mental events are not disentangled from material and bodily structures. Still, they do not emerge from different substances. Without material events, there can be no mental events. Both actually *emerge* from complex levels of organization and encapsulation of material data and information, such as DNA, neurons, and biological and social structures.

Thus, rational behaviour and cognition do not emerge from substantial dualist systems. The idea that the body is merely life support or solely a platform can no longer be proven right. In this sense, Cartesian dualism is an incorrect approach to the mind-body problem. To address the mind-body problem in Cartesian terms means to miss the opportunity to address that problem correctly.

Human bodies are actively engaged in cognitive processes, from the simplest to the most complex paths of rational behaviour. They act upon the emergence of mental events. It is impossible to perceive the emergence of complex rationality without direct engagement of the entire human body. Therefore, bodies are not mere platforms or substances used to enable an immaterial self to develop itself. They *are* expressions of personhood; they are part of human rationality.

If Cartesian language is discontinued when analysing problems related to minds and bodies, nature versus nurture debates are simpler to supersede.

2.4 Nature and culture: superseding the dichotomy

Dichotomy between nature and culture tends to, on the one hand, connect innate skills and core biology to the concept of "nature" and, on the other hand, associate social or constructed skills with the cultural sphere. Consequently, nature and culture can be established only as different and disentangled phenomena.

Thus, human skills can be separated into two types: innate, biologically given skills, and learned, or culturally situated skills. One example regularly used to present the nature versus nurture debate is the difference between walking and cycling:

> [i]t is generally accepted that bipedal locomotion is a universal human characteristic, whose evolution entailed a distinctive suite of anatomical adjustments. Cycling, by contrast, is an acquired skill which has appeared relatively lately in some, but not all, human populations (…). [I]t entailed no reconfiguration of human anatomy (…). [T]he bicycle was designed to 'fit' a human body that had already evolved for walking, and its essential mechanical function is to convert bipedal into rotary motion. (Ingold 2000, p. 374)

In this particular case, human bodies are considered to be equipped with the skill of walking. Cycling must be culturally acquired as a product of adjustment. Therefore, riding a bicycle is understood as a conversion of walking through cultural inputs. In this sense, tool-requiring skills or techniques would not involve adaptation of the human body to a new activity because they are not natural but cultural. This idea, regardless its popularity, is extremely imprecise.

The processes of both walking and cycling are environmentally assembled. To master the skill of bipedal walking, children need to encapsulate complex knowledge. They must *learn* how to walk to do so properly. Human adults who have already learned the skill must pass this information along to children in proper space and time. If walking were an innate skill, (i) infants would be born able to walk, and (ii) any children would be able to walk, regardless of contexts. Because both are false, it is impossible to ascribe bipedalism "to the human organism unless the environmental context enters into the specification of what that organism is." (Ingold 2000, p. 375)

Cycling is, nonetheless, undeniably trickier that walking. Like walking, it requires both bodies and environments. However, another element is essential: the bicycle. Although bicycles are pivotal to the skill of cycling, it does not follow that riding one is a skill that depends solely on the bicycle itself. Cycling is not a mere adaptation of walking, but another skill that must be properly learned.

The signs of both skills are embodied. They change the way bodies work, perhaps permanently. The common notion that *once you have learned how to ride a bike, you will never forget it* is a basic example of this idea: riding a bike, like walking, changes body organization. Neurotransmission, muscles, regular balance and spatial orientation are rearranged to facilitate this new skill.

Body stimuli and environment couple themselves in a two-way interaction. Thus, it does not matter whether human beings belong to the same species, or are genetically similar: diverse environments and skills – such as reading, speaking, logic, cycling, and walking – redesign human beings. Body functions are altered; recruitment of neurons is plastically reorganised. It follows that a determined human being in space, time and circumstances A differs from another human being in space, time and circumstances B. Contemporary neuroscience is now able to demonstrate this idea empirically.

2.5 Plasticity

The human body codifies whole information into action. Nevertheless, the nervous system and brain are the most complex and crucial items of this embodied cognition. We now turn our analysis to these entities.

Brain function and its importance to the concept of mind has ling been a subject of scientific and philosophical investigation. Two main approaches have been developed regarding the character of brains. On the one hand, brains are thought to be static and highly specialized during life. Accordingly, specific brain areas are responsible for specific patterns of behaviour.

On the other hand, following Ivan Pavlov's legacy, brains are often considered *tabula rasa*, that is, "it is in a blank state at birth and thereafter totally at the mercy of its environment" (Bunge 2010, p. 163).

Contemporary cognitive neuroscience, however, states that both approaches are false. Brains are neither static nor blank. They are, in fact, plastic. Several pieces of evidence indicate brains are mouldable and flexible. They are adaptive and are able to change throughout their use.

New neuronal simulations emerge when brains are immersed and absorb different tasks or skills through reorganization of cortical neurons and neuronal multitasking. Therefore, brains are not static. They change according to stimuli, such as narratives of episodic memories or assimilation of artificial tools/engines. The constructive character of episodic memory was essential evidence to the thesis of the plasticity of brains, according to Mario Bunge (2010). Episodic memories are, briefly, memories of previously occurring facts or events. Once thought to be descriptive, episodic memories are actually constructive.

When someone says that an object is "round, red and made out of wood", one can say that the person has just given a raw *description* of an object. However, when someone narrates an event, such as a violent car accident, the person reconstructs the event when recounting it. In other words, the narrator *constructs* the description.

The latter is an exemplification of how brains work to systemise and produce narratives:

> [w]hen recalling episodes, we often combine different memories rather that faithfully reproducing what really happened. To put it in neural terms, the recall of an event often consists in the aggregation of different memory traces. (Bunge 2010, p. 164)

Activities directly involved in what humans tend to label "rationality", such as language[9], decision-making and use of memory, rely upon brain plasticity.

Brain plasticity is also supported through the changeability of bodily representation and image through time. Bodily image and senses of self are, obviously, mediated by brains. It has recently been discovered, however, that brains not only mediate those senses but also recreate them in several distinct ways throughout life due to brain plasticity. One important study has ratified this hypothesis: the case of absorption of artificial tools into the neuronal representation of one's body.

Most research regarding human cognition is not actually conducted with human subjects. Instead, studies are usually carried out through animal experimentation. Monkeys and primates are thus regularly used in cognitive research. These were the models used in a pioneering Japanese investigation of brain plasticity (Iriki/Sakura 2008, pp. 2229–2241).

Iriki and Sakura (2008), of the RIKEN Brain Science Institution trained macaque monkeys to use tools, such as rakes or spoons – a skill not observed in the wild. Following the acquisition of this new skill, scientists observed neurophysiologic responses and molecular genetic and morphological changes within the monkeys' brains.

---

9 Already explored in this paper, *cf.* Section 3.2.

The results were that the simple introduction of basic tools for everyday use enabled animals – and humans – to reshape body image, once the visual receptive field expanded along with tool use. When using tools, the neuronal body image of the macaque monkeys was extended to the tool radius. Thus, external objects – from the simplest to the most complex – *are* reconceived as belonging to one's body. Thereby, "tool use may lead to the ability to *disembody* the sense of self from the literal flesh-and-blood boundaries of one's skin." (Iriki/Sakura 2008, p. 2232)

Thus, plasticity enables brains to assimilate contexts and new technologies to senses of body and self. Both notoriously affect mental states and events – which are undeniably embodied.

2.6 Body and mind as material processes

Changeability is one of the most remarkable features of matter. Matter entails energy, and energy is frame-dependent[10]. As shown above, the character of minds and bodies is changeable throughout life and is frame-dependent. Ultimately, minds and bodies *are* material phenomena.

Bodies are reshaped and redesigned by information, biology, acquisition of skills and social contexts at neurological, molecular and morphological levels. Mind, in turn, is not merely dependent upon matter. Minds *are* embodied matter. As shown above, the notion of mental states and events cannot emerge without material contexts. In this sense, it is impossible to draw a picture of the mind-body problem without the language of materialism. Body and mind are both material phenomena.

These categorizations represent two ways of describing the process of the emergence of rationality from the mediation between humans and the environment. As Tim Ingold asserts, "[b]ody and mind, after all, are not two separate things but two ways of describing the same thing – or, better, the same process – namely the environmentally situated activity of the human organism-person" (Ingold 2000, p. 171).

On the one hand, bodies shall not be considered to be hosts of an immaterial rational mind. Bodies are actively engaged in rationality. On the other hand, minds are seen neither as merely inside the head nor out in the immaterial world. They are "immanent in the active, perceptual engagement of organism and environment" (Ingold 2000, p. 171).

10 Here we adopt the concept of matter as developed by physicist and philosopher Mario Bunge. *Cf.* BUNGE. *Matter and…, cit.*, p. 61–69.

In conclusion, if it is possible to understand the mind-body problem, it is through materialism and objectivism.

2.7 Conclusion

In this section, we have shown that minds and bodies are similar processes, although described in different ways. Both are material, plastic and demand a two-way relationship between biology and environmental conditions. They are constructive rather than given processes.

Thus, ontological claims regarding the relation between minds and bodies indicate that mental and bodily events are material. Epistemological claims state the impossibility of understanding the character of minds and bodies by looking solely at them. Both claims leave room for the less traditional hypothesis that cognition is not only bodily embodied but also *extended*.

It is clear that cognition is embodied. Mental processes are bodily processes. However, these activities can emerge only in complex interacting systems. Thus, it is impossible to understand the nature of mental and bodily processes by looking only at bodies – internally – because both depend on the environment to emerge. It is possible to derive from ontological and epistemological claims the view that mental processes are not assigned to the borders of the biological body. Rather, given the importance of the environment in the emergence of cognition, mental processes would not be restricted to an individual's skin and skull because the environment is not passive, but active. In short, this is the claim that gives rise to the extended mind hypothesis, or active externalism.

3. Extended mind hypothesis

Non-Cartesian concepts of mind tend to consider it to be a material phenomenon. In this section, we discuss two of the most prominent responses to the mind-body problem in non-Cartesian terms: the embodied mind and the extended mind.

3.1 The embodied mind

The common view of the embodied mind indicates that mental processes are constituted by bodily structures, such as the brain, nervous system, and muscles. However, environment plays a passive role with regard to mental processes. Environment, although important, is not considered to be a true element of the emergence of mental states once they are embodied. Therefore, mental states should be located only inside the human body – especially in the brain and nervous system.

According to António Damasio, although brains are essential to the idea of a conscious mind, "body-brain communication goes both ways, from body to brain and in reverse." (Damasio, 2010, p. 174)

Two-way communication between brains and bodies means that neural and chemical signals are constantly sent to the brain, from reactions directly linked to the nervous system to states of muscular contraction and temperature of numerous bodily regions. Even small events that might seem irrelevant to mental processes count. Therefore, Damasio believes that the mind is embodied.

The idea that the mind couples itself to the body is also essential to Lawrence Shapiro. According to him, without the adequate recruitment of the body as a whole, mental processes are incomplete because bodies are not neutral vessels of minds:

> [v]ision for human beings is a process that includes features of the human body (...). Perceptual processes include and depend on bodily structures. This means that a description of various perceptual capacities cannot maintain body neutrality and it also means that an organism with a non-human body will have non-human visual and auditory psychologies. (Shapiro 2004, p. 190)

In summary, the embodied mind hypothesis requires that (i) mental processes be material, (ii) mental processes depend on bodily structures and (iii) there be no human mental processes outside human bodies. The place where mental processes occur does matter in this sense.

3.2 The extended mind hypothesis

Some authors[11] maintain that the embodied mind hypothesis is partially correct. Actually, superseding mind-body dualism through the hypothesis that some mental processes are embodied is somewhat settled in non-Cartesian sciences of mind.

Nevertheless, in accordance with Neil Levy, if we ought to assume that mind also comprises body elements beyond the brain, the soundness of the embodied argument is diminished. For if the mind extends to body elements, such as skin and muscles, there is little evidence that it does not extend *beyond* the human body. Thus,

> if we are forced to admit that mind can extend beyond the skull and into the body, there is little – except prejudice – preventing us from extending it still further. If mind does not have to be entirely an affair of neurons and neurotransmitters, if it can encompass muscular tension or heart rate, then why not electronic pulses or marks on paper as well? (Levy 2007, p. 33)

11 Such as Neil Levy and Mark Rowlands.

The claim that *some* mental processes are partially spread in the environment, namely, beyond the boundaries of skin and skull, is the centre of the extended mind hypothesis[12].

Far from being uncontroversial, the extended mind hypothesis comprises the idea that the mind is not entirely constrained within the human body but instead extends to the environment. The mind, as the set of elements that makes beings rational, "is not limited to the internal resources made up of neurons and neurotransmitters. Instead, it includes the set of tools we have developed for ourselves" (Levy 2007, p. 29).

Andy Clark and David Chalmers, philosophers of mind, developed the classical version of the extended mind hypothesis. Both authors state that *some* mental events, such as belief-based cognition, can be environmentally dependent. For example, if a man suffering from Alzheimer's disease learns that the Museum of Modern Art is located on the 53rd Street by consulting his notebook (or his new smartphone), and a woman without the disease internally remembers the same address (from a memory-based cognition), then the location of cognition is irrelevant. Both processes of belief cognition are mental – no matter where they are located. In summary, this is the Otto-Inga thought experiment described by Clark and Chalmers (Clark/Chalmers 2010, p. 27–31).

The extended mind hypothesis confers weight on the external world as the source of cognition and storage of important information for the emergence of personhood. Due to this importance, at least some mental processes are, as Mark Rowlands noted, hybrid: they can occur inside and outside the human body (Rowlands 2004, p. 28). The mind is thus extended if the environment plays an active role in driving mental processes, such as decision-making, language codification and morality. The coupling between human beings and the environment is mentally significant if human action upon the environment changes (material property) something that is merely in the outside world into available knowledge to be strategically used by this agent.

This idea leads to the conclusion that the epistemological claim of the extended mind hypothesis is that it is possible to understand only some mental processes as a hybrid two-way interaction between a cognizing organism and its environment. We note, however, that no matter how important environments are, no form of the extended mind hypothesis maintains that cognition is only outside of humans.

12 We note that the term "extended mind" is the most traditional nomenclature of this view, although many other authors label it differently. The very authors who called it "extended mind" once named it "active externalism". Mark Rowlands (2004) calls it environmentalism. The present texts will focus on the most prominent.

To state that some mental processes are hybrid is not the same as stating that they depend upon the environment. Dependence upon the environment can be seen at the embodied mind hypothesis. The extended mind goes further because it asserts that environmental aspects compose some mental processes and that composition differs from dependence (Rowlands 2010, p. 60). The guiding principle of the extended mind is the irrelevance of boundaries between internal and external worlds. It focuses on the *role* played by some element, not on the location of the element. In this sense,

> [i]f, as we confront some task, a part of the world functions as a process which, *were it done in the head*, we would have no hesitation in accepting as part of the cognitive process, then that part of the world is (so we claim) part of the cognitive process. (Clark/Chalmers 2010, p. 29)

Finally, this hypothesis makes claims about the character of mental processes. Thus, some processes are composed of transforming or manipulating environmental structures (Rowlands 2010, p. 67).

This notion does not mean that cognitive processes are *identical* to environmental structures because this is not relevant to the emergence of mind. What ultimately matters is the role that environmental structures play when manipulated by cognizing organisms. This role can be displayed only if the cognizing organism and the environment are coupled in parity conditions. If an external feature plays some role that, were it internal, would clearly be mental, then there is nothing preventing us from calling it mental.

Finally, according to Neil Levy, if this is the case, then the location of the process – bodily or environmentally restricted – is ethically irrelevant: "[s]ince the mind extends into the external environment, alterations of external props used for thinking are (*ceteris paribus*) ethically on a par with alterations on the brain." (Levy 2007, p. 61)Brain plasticity and the adaptive character of human cognition are two key features contained in the extended mind hypothesis.

3.3 Conclusion

In the present section, we sought to prove that mental processes are hybrid[13], meaning that they take place partially in both bodies and environments. Accordingly, mental processes would be embodied *and* extended. Still, considering the hybrid character of minds, it follows that composition of cognitive elements such as beliefs, desires and behaviours, is extremely diffuse. There is little space for

13 For hybridism of mental processes, see Rowlands 2010.

a priori definition of the character of cognition anterior to the affectedness between bodies and environments.

Therefore, mental processes could be described as not strictly assignable to the brain or even the body of a cognizing organism. They are increasingly spread in cognitive environments and coupled to tools that make life less costly for those organisms.

The mind-body problem, in accordance with the view held in this paper, shall not be answered from a Cartesian-dualist standpoint. Rather, the answer to the problem must be functionalist. The extended mind hypothesis, or active externalism, offers a functionalist account of the mind-body problem, which includes another core element: the environment. In this regard, what makes a particular process mental is not the location at which it is elaborated. It is the role that it plays, i.e., the function performed by mental processes. If a certain mental process involves a cognitive framework, it matters little whether it is attached to the body or is partially outside it.

Empiricism and objectivity, therefore, demand that we abandon the language commonly used to provide answers to the mind-body problem. Transition from the Cartesian-dualist response to Functional Externalism has several repercussions in Western Legal Sciences. Concepts such as autonomy, responsibility, decision-making and, finally, the very notion of persons and legal institutions are thoroughly shattered by the abandonment of internalism.

4. Law and hybrid cognition

The previous sections have sought to debunk the notion of mind-body dualism. It has been demonstrated that cognition and emergence of rational behaviour are predominantly hybrid processes. Accordingly, alterations in bodies and environments result in reformulations of both mental processes and subjects. This idea, apparently simple, impacts fields such as Law.

Nevertheless, changes in subjects, however technological and innovative they may seem, are not new. Beneficial changes, such as human enhancement, have been occurring for thousands of years by means of mastery and redefinition of environments and bodies.

This concept applies, for example, to the formal education process to which human beings have been submitted throughout the last few thousand years. Education is indeed not an innate, but a dialogic process. It is a form of human enhancement aimed at expending a person's horizons of meaning and action. Changes, however, do not stop at the bodies of subjects. They also alter the environment, generating globally enhanced societies – as education does.

Although enhancements are not new or recent in human history, contemporary technologies increase the possibility of creating or altering legal subjects. These technologies are so vast and powerful that they can transform mental states that have existed for years, such as depression or compulsion. Hybrid technologies, such as brain implants (chips), brain-machine interfaces, genetic alterations and use of cognitive drugs redefine the frontiers of traditional legal subjects, such as the human being. Hybrid technologies are, in this sense, actual technologies of autonomy because they allow subjects to pursue broader ideals of a good life. Interaction between bodies and environments through technology lead to creation of values, which, in turn, modify neuronal emergence due to brain plasticity.

Consequences of changes in the language used to address mental, bodily and environmental issues can be seen in the form through which Law addresses with concepts such as autonomy and legal institutions, such as prison systems. Embedding technologies in people's daily lives can be seen as enhancing their autonomy. The use of psychopharmaceutical drugs, for example, can be understood as an autonomy booster because it allows a person to experience a broader sense of action.

Furthermore, the role of the environment in the construction of a subject's sense of self, for example, is pivotal. Innumerable experiments stress the importance of informational environments to the process of decision-making. One is the Stanford Prison Experiment. In this controversial social experiment, scientists led by Philip Zimbardo recruited twenty-four male students. The students were divided into two groups, prisoners and guards, and received strategies for behaviour control.

During the experiment, the prisoners went through a process of deep depersonalization and, on the second day of confinement, exhibited odd patterns of behaviour. The guards also changed their behaviour quickly through the use of psychological and physical violence to discipline prisoners. According to Zimbardo, the "extent of creative evil in which many of the guards engaged, [and the] extent of the suffering of many of the prisoners" was painful (Zimbardo, Philip: *The Lucifer effect: understanding how good people turn evil.* Random House Trade Paperback: New York 2008, p. IX).

The experiment indicated that individual actions are environment-dependent and can originate outside subjects. In this sense, it is impossible to understand the decision-making process by looking exclusively at individuals' internal processes. Rationality and cognition are, in conclusion, conditional on biology, institutions, information and environments, as are persons and new forms of personhood. In this sense, to deliberate on the legal approach to autonomy, responsibility and institutionalization of behaviours is ultimately to consider the hybridism of mental processes.

References

Bechara, Antoine. Tranel, Daniel. Damasio, Hanna (2000): 'Characterization of the decision-making deficit of patients with ventromedial prefrontal cortex'. *Brain* 123, pp. 2189–2202.

Bechara, Antoine *et al. 1998)*: 'Dissociation of working memory from decision making within the human prefrontal cortex'. *The Journal of Neuroscience* 18 (1), pp. 428–437.

Bunge, Mario (2010): *Matter and mind: a philosophical inquiry* (Boston Studies in the Philosophy of Science 287). Springer: Dordrecht *et al.*

Bunge, Mario: "Emergence and the mind". *Neuroscience* 2 (4), 1977, pp. 501–509.

Crane, Tim/Patterson, Sarah: *History of the mind-body problem*. Routledge: London 2002.

Damasio, António R. (2010): *Self comes to mind: constructing the conscious brain*. Pantheon Books: New York.

Damasio, António R. (1994): *Descartes' error: emotion, reason and the human brain*. Avon Books: New York.

Descartes, René: *Discourse on method of rightly conducting one's reason and of seeking truth in the sciences* [Kindle Edition]. Retrieved from Amazon.

Descartes, René: *Meditations on first philosophy. With selections from the objections and replies*. Oxford University Press: Oxford 2008.

Ingold, Tim (2000): *The perception of environment: essays on livelihood, dwelling and skill*. Routledge: London.

Iriki, Atsushi, Sakura, Osamu (2008): 'The neuroscience of primate intellectual evolution: natural selection and passive and intentional niche construction'. *Philosophical Transactions of the Royal Society B: Biological Sciences* 363 (1500), pp. 2229–2241.

Levy, Neil (2007): *Neuroethics: challenges for the 21st century*. Cambridge University Press: Cambridge *et al.*

Menary, Richard Ed. (2010): *The extended mind*. The MIT Press: Cambridge *et al.*

Rowlands, Mark: *The new science of the mind: from extended mind to embodied phenomenology*. The MIT Press: Cambridge *et al.* 2010.

Rowlands, Mark (2004): *The body in mind: understanding cognitive processes* (Cambridge Studies in Philosophy). Cambridge University Press: Cambridge.

Shapiro, Lawrence (2004): *The mind* incarnate. The MIT Press: Cambridge *et al.*

Stich, Stephen P., Warfield, Ted A. (2003): *The Blackwell Guide to the Philosophy of Mind*. Blackwell Publishing: Oxford.

Wolf, Maryanne (2008): *Proust and the squid: the story and science of the reading brain*. Harper Perennial: New York.

Zimbardo, Philip (2008): *The Lucifer effect: understanding how good people turn evil*. Random House Trade Paperback: New York.

Malte-Christian Gruber

Legal Subjects and Partial Legal Subjects in Electronic Commerce

1. Starting Points: Legal Capacities and Partial Legal Capacities

1.1 Intermediate stages of legal capacity

> Legal capacity can be defined within the meaning of modern jurisprudence as the ability to enter into relations guaranteed by existing law and the opportunity thereby bestowed to enjoy legally protected advantage. But this is a rather vague, vacuous definition. However, it shares this fate with all definitions of basic legal concepts, such as those of property, family, liberty and civil rights. All of these cases, like that of legal capacity, involve social institutions that were not created in one go but look back on a thousand-year history, and continue to bear some of the marks of each intermediate stage of their entire development to the present day. To describe the handiwork on which so many countless generations have hammered and chiseled in a few words is, needless to say, a task that can be performed only in an extremely deficient way. (Ehrlich 1909/1973, p. 1)

Eugen Ehrlich, the author of these introductory words, liberates legal scholars from exaggerated expectations concerning what they can accomplish in their conceptual and systematic work. That basic legal concepts such as legal capacity can be defined unambiguously may be a necessary assumption of legal dogmatics; but when faced with the living law of social relations, this assumption proves to be an illusion. Although one could extend the faith in progress of our technological – in particular, information technological – age to jurisprudence and hope that it has in the meantime found a more precise version, the opposite is more likely to be the case. Also over the course of the century since Ehrlich's work *Die Rechtsfähigkeit* (*Legal Capacity*), jurisprudence has not matured to such an extent that it does not embarrass itself time and again.[1]

What provokes legal embarrassment nowadays in defining legal capacity, however, is not so much the history examined by Rudolf von Jhering (1857, p. 16), but the new technological and social challenges that even millennia of

1 It may be true, as Rudolf von Jhering (1857, p. 16) has pointed out, that a "mature jurisprudence" is immune to embarrassment by history. But it nonetheless remains indebted to its social (as well as non-social) environments. See Rudolf Wiethölter 1992, p. 226.

work in jurisprudence cannot anticipate. The resulting controversies over the legal status of human life in the peripheral areas of human existence (cf. Gruber 2003, pp. 135–140), the question of the rights of non-human organisms and other entities (cf. Teubner 2006; Gruber 2006), as well as the recent changes in the law of partnerships (Reuter 2007; Beuthien 2011), contribute in different ways to the concept of legal capacity seeming, if anything, even more vague and fragmented than in Ehrlich's time.

In this respect, the recent development of social institutions, in particular of concepts of legal capacity and hence also of legal subjectivity or of legal personality (cf. Reuter 2007, p. 674 and 687–697), seems to represent a continuation of the gradual development through intermediate stages described by Ehrlich. As tokens of these intermediate stages, the concepts of partial legal capacity and, correspondingly, of partial legal subjectivity, which will be examined more closely in what follows with reference to new forms of attribution of agency and identity in electronic commerce, are also part of the currently observable "limits of law." These are shown in the already widely-diagnosed symptoms of disintegration of traditional conceptual dichotomies, in the inadequacies of binary-coded law in the face of the many new challenges of its social environment, and, finally, also in the formation of new legal concepts and constructions in an attempt to cope better with these challenges in future.

1.2 Participation in the law and legal protection

If we take another, closer look at the opening quotation from Eugen Ehrlich, we can nevertheless already identify two important elements of legal capacity in the definition he describes as "vague" and "vacuous": first, the ability to enter into legal relations, and, second, the possibility of enjoying legally protected advantage or, in other words, legal protection.

The first element, participation in legal relations, points to the well-known premise formulated by Savigny (1840, § 60, p. 1) that every legal relation involves a relationship between one person and another person. This is based in turn on the Kantian definition that a "*person* is a subject whose actions can be *imputed* to him." (Kant 1797/1996, p. 16 [Ak. 6:223]). Even though by "person" and "subject" here are meant, of course, only human beings who are accountable – that is, who are able to act under binding laws of the categorical imperative – this already involves a functional reorientation of the concept of the person. Subjects are no longer the bearers of their actions without further qualification only because they exhibit certain characteristics such as the ability to reason or simple physical mobility. Rather, they are first *regarded* as authors of their actions and their effects;[2] actions are attributed to them. This shift in perspective to one of attribution opens the legal conceptions of personality and responsibility, and hence of agency and legal capacity, to a functionalist approach for which it has long since ceased to be mandatory that only human individuals should be considered to be bearers of rights and duties (cf. Raiser 1999, pp. 118f.; Teubner 1987, pp. 61ff.; id. 2006, pp. 497ff.; Gruber 2009, pp. 299ff.).

Somewhat more contentious, by contrast, is the question whether Ehrlich's second, abstractly formulated element of legal capacity – the granting of legally protected advantage – is exclusively a product of the attributions of observers. It is already a different matter, and constitutes an additional qualitative step, if, instead of concentrating on mere participation in legal relationships, one also speaks of the opportunity to enjoy legal advantages. This apparently no longer only concerns the question of being a legal entity, but rather a claim to legal protection that must actually be realized. And this impinges on a particular aspect of legal capacity which is no longer simply a matter of rights, but of "rights to rights" (see Arendt 1955, p. 476) – in other words, protection of dignity, and if necessary legal recognition of personality (Gruber 2013, pp. 417ff.).

One would like to think that such specific definitions of legal capacity are restricted to human beings, or at least to living beings. They alone should be attributed dignity, moreover unreservedly, absolutely. Therefore, it is at first sight counterintuitive also to make this aspect of legal subjectivity dependent on the standpoint of an attributing observer. Note, however, that this only involves a specific aspect of legal subjectivity that exhibits a special relation to human beings qua social beings and simultaneously qua extra-social, living individuals. This in no way contradicts the idea that legal capacity exhibits many different intermediate stages and can also be attributed in corresponding ways to nonhuman subjects. Both the ability to participate in legal relationships as well as the claim to legal protection exist in incremental gradations as regards their content and their scope (cf. Gruber 2013, pp. 417ff.; see also id. 2006, pp. 160ff.).

Eugen Ehrlich (1909/1973, pp. 1f.) refers in this connection primarily to the individual components of human legal capacity, in particular to the variable, historically contingent limitations of political rights, family rights, property rights

---

2 See Kant, loc. cit.: "An action is called a *deed* insofar as it comes under obligatory laws and hence insofar as the subject, in doing it, is considered in terms of the freedom of his choice. By such an action the agent is regarded as the *author* of its effect, and this, together with the action itself, can be *imputed* to him, if one is previously acquainted with the law by virtue of which an obligation rests on these."

and personal rights. Entirely new intermediate stages are added with the theory of the legal person (cf. Beuthien 2011, pp. 124ff.; Raiser 1999, pp. 104ff.), and more recently by the rulings on the limited legal capacity[3] and the partial legal capacity[4] of partnerships and associations. The extension of legal capacity in the domain of company law in particular shows the effects of the social practice of treating partnerships as "living law" and how this has led first law-makers and subsequently jurisdiction to reassess legal capacity (Reuter 2007, pp. 674–680). Civil law partnerships and other bodies of persons functioned as collective social actors with their own social address and identity long before the introduction of section 14 (2) BGB (German Civil Code), for example, with its definition of legal partnerships,[5] and before the related rulings on "partial legal capacity" became possible.

However, the concept of "partial legal capacity" is not only applicable to bodies of persons. Corresponding transitional stages can already be found at the limits of the personal existence of individual human beings. Thus, the conceived but still unborn human being is partially legal capable from the moment of conception on in so far as, for example, it is already regarded in this situation as capable of inheriting (section 1923 (2) BGB) and enjoys protection under civil law against prenatal damage to health (section 823 (1) BGB) (cf. Gruber 2003, pp. 135–138).

Moreover, with the increasing possibilities of medical technology, there seems to be a simultaneous increase in the difficulties in defining a clear beginning and end point of the personal existence of human beings, and thus in defining their legal subjectivity. Even the legal treatment of the time of birth is inconsistent. In addition, new findings concerning the prenatal status of human beings, as well as doubts concerning the brain death criterion and uncertainties in dealing with human beings in a persistent vegetative state, are leading to a further multiplication of incremental attributions of personality (cf. Ulsenheimer 2007; Müller 2010; see also Eisenberg 2008; Farah 2008; Varelius 2009).

In this context, it is also becoming apparent that there is not just one, but many legal capacities, whose scope can be more or less restricted. There are

---

3 Cf. German Federal Supreme Court (Bundesgerichtshof), BGHZ 146, 341, at 344 ("limited legal subjectivity" of partnerships under the German Civil Code); for further enhancements of legal subjectivity, see BGHZ 148, 291; 154, 88; 154, 370, as well as BGH NJW 2006, 3716; 2007, 995; 2008, 1378; 2009, 594; 2011, 615; 2011, 1958; 2011, 2048; BGH NJW 2007, 2490; 2011, 1595.

4 BGHZ 163, 154 (partial legal capacity of condominium association).

5 Section 14 (2) BGB, introduced on 30 June 2000 (BGBl. I 897): "A partnership with legal personality is a partnership that has the capacity to acquire rights and to incur liabilities."

correspondingly many types of legal subjects and partial legal subjects, and ever-new types can develop, at the latest once the law confronts new social and technological challenges. Today such challenges seem to be making themselves felt especially in the field of information and communication technologies.

2. Extensions: Legal Subjectivity in Electronic Commerce

2.1 Legal constructions in the domain of information technology

To date, however, the concept of partial legal capacity does not seem to play any significant role in information technology law. In this area, the dissolution of conceptual dichotomies is more likely to come from the other side of the subject-object dualism: the "partial objectification" of Internet domains is thematized as the mirror-image counterpart of partial legal subjectivity, as it were (Krebs/Becker 2009, p. 934), or also the legal status of virtual objects "in the gray area between real things and pure rights." (Spindler 2011a; see also Berberich 2010) This makes it clear, at any rate, that information technology law seems to be compelled to experiment with new "thing concepts," for example, those of "boundary objects" or "quasi-objects." (cf. Latour 1993, pp. 49ff. et passim; on these concepts, see Roßler 2008, pp. 76ff.).

Again, the conceptual and constructive innovations can be interpreted as responses to new social challenges to which the law now finds itself exposed in the technologized world of new information technology communications media. These challenges are a result in particular of the fact that meaningful and technological communication are becoming visibly amalgamated in the information technology media (cf. Vesting 2003, p. 179). This is shown, for example, by the fact that software codes are now virtually indistinguishable from intellectual content (Bullinger/Czychowski 2011, pp. 19ff.), or that intellectual property as well as information technology systems seem to be simultaneously part of social communication and of the personal development of human users[6] – in short, that the clear separation between the "internal" world of the personal legal subject and the "external" world of available legal objects and items of property is breaking down.

To this extent, information technologies can no longer be qualified exclusively as "external," purely technical environments of communication, but constitute beyond that a new kind of social domain. Its peculiarities are already a product, on the one hand, of the actual behavior of human users, who are increasingly

6 See, in particular, German Federal Constitutional Court (Bundesverfassungsgericht) BVerfGE 120, 274 ("Online-Durchsuchung").

bound, both cognitively and emotionally, into information technology systems at a psychosocial level. On the other hand, it is also the special material conditions of information technology communications systems in particular that lead human persons who are under their influence to appear as new functional units composed of body, mind and artificial medium. The networked communication medium "computer" is playing a major role in shaping the conditions of social communication based on its technical specifications in the form of digital codes, programming languages, user interfaces and text formats (Vesting 2003, pp. 179–181).

These specific communicative conditions of social information technologies resulting from the technological networking of social communication have a particularly pronounced influence on legal attributions of identity and action, and hence above all on issues of liability in electronic commerce. Here in particular it is becoming increasingly difficult to distinguish concrete human actors and, for example, to identify them as authors of declarations of intent or even as individually responsible agencies of legal transgressions. The communicative processes in this area appear instead as new kinds of chains of effects whose actors seem to be more socio-technical ensembles of people and things – whereby the artificial components of these hybrid human being-thing linkages can sometimes even be represented as driving forces and independent agents.

2.2 Extensions of liability through information technology

Such hybrid linkages between humans and non-human systems can be found not only in the visions of especially future-oriented information technologies, such as the latest developments in the "Internet of things and services" and in the field of "ambient intelligence," "ambient assisted living" or "cyber-physical systems" (Herzog *et al.* 2009, p. 11). In everyday electronic commerce there are already numerous cases all of which raise the question, in a way that is in principle comparable, of individual liability for technological and for the most part automated processes, thus for communicative processes which, from a human perspective, are scarcely possible to control any more. These cases involve, for example, the abuse of user accounts, Wi-Fi connections, auction platforms or forums by third parties, whose identity cannot be ascertained for the most part. As a result, liability claims for legal infringements can be asserted only against the respective operators.

To what extent the latter can be held liable for damages, injunctive relief and removal in individual cases regularly depends on whether it can be proved that they acted with intent qua accomplices or participants with respect to the infringement. For the numerous cases in which this cannot be proven, however, legal jurisdiction has developed in addition the construct of indirect liability for interference

("Störerhaftung") in the domain of intellectual property law. According to this construct, injunctive relief and removal can be sought also from those operators on the grounds that they are "interferers" who contribute to the legal infringement through no fault of their own, yet in an adequate causal way, by violating a duty to examine. To what extent the operators can reasonably be expected to fulfill such duties to examine and act and to what extent these duties can be considered to be proportionate depends on the details of each case.[7]

Given the large number of such individual cases that have been adjudicated in the meantime, it is virtually impossible to derive any reliable standards from legal rulings. At any rate, a certain understanding of the technological context is required. Assertions about the reasonableness of duties to examine can be made only on an "expert" basis. Such duties can be judged only within the framework of the existing technological possibilities that are apt to prevent an interference. However, in their assessments of the duties to act that can be reasonably expected in concrete cases, and especially their probability assessments of opportunities for abuse and prevention, the courts often rely on their own expertise and the rules of prima facie evidence based on this (cf. Hoeren 2008, p. 2618). This shift in liability law to the assessment of evidence and case-by-case decision-making by judges means that the corresponding attributions of agency and responsibility for the conduct of third parties can occur within a wide latitude of "adequate causality".

But even beyond these extended liability standards, the courts are continually finding new, constructive paths of attribution. In the case of anticompetitive practices[8] and now also of infringements of intellectual property,[9] jurisdiction has even taken to dealing with the responsible operators as direct infringers, and hence as perpetrators of the violations of competition law and property rights committed by third parties. According to the so-called "Halzband" decision[10] of the Federal Court of Justice (BGH) of 2009, the duties of care of holders of eBay member accounts are especially far-reaching. In the case in question, the Latvian spouse of the defendant had offered her necklace at a minimum bid of 30 euros through his eBay account, among other things, with the garbled words: "SSSuper ... Tolle ... Halzband (Cartier Art)" and "... Halzband, Art Cartier ... Mit kl. Pantere, tupische simwol fon Cartier Haus ... [SSSuper ... great ... necklace (Cartier

7 Cf., in particular, BGHZ 158, 236 ("Internet-Versteigerung I"); BGHZ 148, 13 ("ambiente.de"); BGH GRUR 2011, 152, 154ff. ("Kinderhochstühle im Internet"); on the development of the so-called "interferer's liability" ("Störerhaftung"), see Spindler 2011b.

8 Cf. BGHZ 173, 188 ("Jugendgefährdende Medien bei eBay").

9 Cf. BGHZ 180, 134 ("Halzband").

10 BGHZ 180, 134.

style) … necklace, Cartier style … with small pantere, tipical simwol fron Cartier house …]" The court took the view that the defendant had committed a breach of duty by failing to adequately protect the secrecy[11] of his login data. This represents an independent ground of attribution compared to the principles of liability for interference in the area of intellectual property law as well as duties of care in competition law:

> If a third party uses another member's account on eBay, having come into possession of the login data to this account because the holder of the account failed to protect them sufficiently against access by third parties, the holder of the member account must be treated as if he had acted himself. … The reason for the liability of those who have failed to keep their contact information secure resides … in the danger they create that confusion could arise for commerce over which person has traded under the eBay member account, and that as a result the possibilities of identifying, and if necessary bringing an action against the agent (whether for injunctive relief or for damages), may be significantly impaired.[12]

If one takes the Federal Court of Justice at its word, then inadequate protection of user account login data automatically entails a fiction of perpetration according to which holders of membership accounts whose access has been abused by third parties are to be treated as if they had acted through this access themselves. Because of the very general terms in which it is formulated, this fictive agency for unsecured eBay accounts seem to be applicable not only to the case of infringements of competition and intellectual property law decided here, but also to numerous other contractual problem cases in electronic commerce in which third parties make declarations of intent and conclude contracts through other people's user accounts. At any rate, the justification presented for the judgment at first sight suggest this in so far as it is not based, for example, on an increased risk of legal infringements, but instead on the interest of those engaged in legal transactions in being able to ascertain clearly the identity of the person acting under the user account in each instance.[13]

It makes sense that those engaged in legal transactions have a particular interest in being able to identify potential business and contractual partners at all times. The identity of the contracting parties belongs as a matter of principle to the essential preconditions of a contractual agreement. If a third party acts under an assumed name, or correspondingly under another person's user account, a liability of the account holder in accordance with principles of prima facie liability comes

11 The defendant had kept his personal access data in his desk which was also accessible to his spouse.

12 BGHZ 180, 134, 139.

13 BGHZ 180, 134, 140.

into consideration (Oechsler 2008).[14] However, liability is ruled out – as the Federal Court of Justice itself noted in the justification of its ruling[15] – in particular if the account holder was not at least able to recognize the action of the unauthorized person, and also if the contractual partner is not worthy of protection, for example because he or she recognized the abuse or negligently failed to recognize it. However, the Federal Court of Justice no longer wants to accept this caveat of a consideration of the protection-worthy interests of both parties for the case of tort liability for violations of property rights. Specifically, individuals who in breach of their duty fail to keep the login data of their eBay accounts secure should not be able to appeal from the outset to an interest that overrides the protection of the legal interests in question.[16]

This weighting of the respective interests may at first sight seem to be irreproachable – breach of duty on the one side, violation of intellectual property rights and rights based on ancillary copyright law on the other side. It is questionable, however, whether this should even turn on the transactional interests, in particular the interests of the parties to a civil liability case. For the evaluation of the legitimate interests of those engaged in legal transactions relating to the identifiability of the actors rests primarily on legal transactional reasons and not on tort-based reasons. What is at stake is in fact the identity of one's contractual partner, because without it no contract can be concluded. In contrast, the identifiability of tort liability opponents against whom actions are to be brought in future is more a matter of the general requirements of preventive prosecution (cf. Leistner 2010, p. 6f.). It may be doubted, therefore, whether a conception of liability for the fraudulent use of user accounts by third parties, comparable to the principles of (legal transactional) prima facie liability,[17] can be applied in the area of torts, and – in the absence of a balancing of interests – whether it can even be extended considerably further in that area. Against such misgivings, the Federal Court of Justice ultimately also cites the interests of the public:

The liability model presented above does not burden the defendant in a disproportionate manner. It merely updates to take account of the new technological developments the principle that persons to whom a legally protected area is allocated for use and, where applicable, also to make a profit are liable within the bounds of their responsibility for this area for legal infringements if they fail in

14 For a different view, see BGH VersR 2011, 932 = NJW 2011, 2421.
15 BGHZ 180, 134, 140f., with further references.
16 BGHZ 180, 134, 141.
17 For such a comparison, see BGHZ 180, 134, 140f.; cf. also Rössel 2009, pp. 453ff.; for a more skeptical view, see Leistner 2010, p. 7.

their duty to provide safeguards in the interest of third parties or of the general public.[18]

Thus the response of the Federal Court of Justice to the new technical developments consists in justifying spheres of responsibility and liability that should correspond in scope to the areas of activity of the user. The court identifies such an area of activity in the access to the eBay user account that, based on monitoring data and password protection, serves as "a special means of identification" whose "identification function … goes far beyond the use of stationery, a name or an address, for example, where it is known to those engaged in commerce that these can, if necessary, be imitated or improperly used by anyone."[19]

There are good reason for doubting whether the Federal Court of Justice makes an accurate assessment of the knowledge of those involved in legal transactions concerning the possibilities of identity fraud using eBay accounts, which can easily be set up at any time under false names and addresses (cf. Hartmann 2011, p. 92). Of much greater import, however, is the constructive step that the court makes at this point by founding a new sphere of technological responsibility. The eBay account holder is liable as the perpetrator of a violation of competition and property law, not, for example, because he has done something, but because an action has been performed in a technical area assigned to his identity.

2.3 "Indirect" perpetrator of the actions of others?

The trends in jurisdiction described towards extending the scope of liability, which have reached a provisional climax in the "Halzband" ruling, suggest that the ascription of responsibilities to individual human beings is becoming increasingly difficult and must sooner or later give rise to an aporia. The aporia is that the perpetrators no longer appear only as the personally responsible authors of their own actions in the traditional sense, but are also at the same time blamed for the deeds that they have not performed, but have been performed by third parties (at their own initiative) – in short, they become perpetrators of the deeds of others.

The looming paradox could be seen at first sight as an exaggerated extrapolation of the problem familiar from discussions in criminal law of the single perpetrator concept in the case of negligence offenses, which does not allow any differentiations with regard to the incrementally different contributions to degrees of completion and to forms of duties of care (cf. Renzikowski 1997, pp. 154ff.).

18 BGHZ 180, 134, 143f.
19 BGHZ 180, 134, 139f.

In parallel to this, tort imputation in civil law[20] also seems to have difficulties in dealing with the multiple linkages between actors and concerned parties that it encounters especially in the social information technologies as "indirect legal infringements" (Leistner 2010, pp. 1ff.).

Thus, the precise legal basis for extending the liability of perpetrators in the "Halzband" case remains unclear to date (Hartmann 2011, p. 92). Strictly speaking, it cannot be based on a violation of extended duties of care (cf. Peifer 2009; Hecht 2009; Leistner 2010), since at the time of the breach of duty – that is, of the inadequate protection of the login data against abuse – a concrete threat of a violation of property rights did not even exist as yet. In any case, the Federal Court of Justice did not want to justify the duty to safeguard login data in terms of an increased threat of legal infringements, but instead in terms of a threat to commerce posed by the potential confusion concerning the identity of the actor.[21] But a corresponding classification as "prima facie tort liability" (Rössel 2009, p. 454) seems unconvincing, especially as the liability is supposed to be affirmed regardless of whether the identity of the actor in fact remained unclear or not for those engaged in commerce (cf. Leistner 2010, p. 6f.). Just as little as the justification of an extended liability for security of commerce can an extended concept of prima facie liability establish an adequate link between the duty to safeguard login data and the danger, which arises – if at all – only later, of a violation of legally protected interests that cannot count as endangered at the time of the breach of duty (cf. Ungern-Sternberg 2010, p. 392).

In light of this, it seems more plausible to appeal to the legal idea of the special statutory rules for imputing liability to the owners of a company or a business for their employees or agents (section 99 UrhG [German Copyright Act], section 14 (7) MarkenG [German Trademark Act], section 8 (2) UWG [German Unfair Competition Act]) (see Ungern-Sternberg, ibid.). Owners should indeed use the division of labor within their company or business to make a profit, but not to shift responsibility for actions to dependent third parties, or even to spread it over the whole collective. The Federal Court of Justice seems to be concerned with a very similar prevention of the delegation or confusion of responsibility in its "Halzband" decision. Here, too, holders of the eBay accounts are not supposed to be able exonerate themselves with the claim – certainly often cited in cases of "indirect" legal infringements – that it was not they themselves but a third party

---

20 Civil liability, especially tortious liability of multiple tortfeasors (according to section 830 BGB), is essentially based on the rules developed by criminal law: cf. BGHZ 63, 124, 126; 89, 383, 389.

21 Cf. BGHZ 180, 134, 140.

who acted through the access (cf. Ungern-Sternberg, ibid.). Succinctly put, as users of the technology they are also liable for the technology.

However, the newly-contrived reason of the Federal Court of Justice for attributing responsibility to eBay account holders who fail to take sufficient measures to protect their login data goes well beyond entrepreneurial liability, since the latter is confined to company- or business-related actions (cf. Leistner 2010, p. 6). In contrast, the liability of eBay account holders is supposed to exist independently of their specific actions and modes of use, based solely on the high "identification function"[22] of the account. As a "legally protected area," this seems to be allocated to the account holder not only, as the Federal Court of Justice points out, "for use and, where applicable, also to make a profit," but also even represents an IT extension of the entire identity of the account holder.

The ever more broadly construed attributions and imputations of responsibility for "indirect" infringement can be justified at first sight only in terms of increasingly extensive duties of care and practical duties or of a prima facie obligation that refers in a peculiar way to commerce in general, or even of an analogy to other special statutory forms of accountability for actions in collective contexts. But behind this there presumably ultimately lurks a far more profound change in a little-questioned basic concept of civil law. According to this, it is no longer individual human beings alone qua isolated subjects to whom actions, intentions, declarations of intent, responsibilities and ultimately rights and duties are ascribed. Rather, their identities augmented by IT artifacts are also prone to lead to a new, extended conception of legal capacity and legal subjectivity.

2.4 Legal subjects associated through information technology

The problems and deficiencies of tort action attribution and their systematic classification make it clear that the traditional model of imputation that takes the individual human being defined as "self-determined" as its point of departure loses its persuasiveness to the extent that – instead of being able to refer back to objective causal relationships and subjective intentions – it increasingly has to contrive breaches of duties and prevention opportunities on a case-by-case basis just in order to identify perpetrators. To all appearances, the individualistic perspective no longer finds any indigenous subjects of action specifically in the increasing interdependencies of information technology in particular, but must first bring its subjects to the action.

---

22 BGHZ 180, 134, 139.

Even though "indirect" liability as a perpetrator for actions that are not one's own may also be a mere fiction, such fictions are the "crutches of thought" in Josef Esser's (1969, p. 200) sense. At any rate, they are always at the same time the harbingers of future legal realities. However, future novel constructions of agency and responsibility are almost impossible to capture adequately in terms of the traditional terminology; what is required, therefore, are new concepts that do better justice to a new legal reality marked by the interdependencies of social information technologies.

From such a perspective, no longer only the human individual identifiable by its self-determined actions and volitions counts as a legal subject. Rather, the person in the IT medium is henceforth also identified with artificial entities, in the "Halzband" case with a password-protected eBay account. Persons can no longer liberate themselves from this widening attribution of identity and action. For example, they can no longer free themselves from the attribution of responsibility for the eBay account by – as in the case of liability for interference – satisfying other reasonable duties to examine directed to a possible prevention of abuse.[23]

Of scant importance here is also whether it was the account holder him or herself or instead a third person who abused the access in order to commit infringements of property rights and breaches of competition law.[24] Once again, it is the attributions of social observers – here of electronic commerce with its specific requirements on the identifiability and addressability of persons – that constitute the legal subject. They determine the degree to which and the limits within which the human person qua subject of liability and attribution is extended. And these extensions reach such a level in the interdependencies of communication and information technologies in particular that human persons are increasingly represented, beyond the boundaries of their biological bodies and their supposedly self-determined will, also as a fixed linkage of human being and things – or, in the words of Bruno Latour, as an "association of humans and non-humans" (Latour 1993, p. 4; see also id. 2005, p. 43ff.).

Of course, these extensions are not cited as such in the legal justifications – and it would be very surprising if they were. Legal dogmatics remains firmly rooted in a conceptual tradition that still speaks of natural persons, self-determination and declarations of intent – in spite of the fact that it should have long since become clear that persons are communicative constructs, that self-determinations rest on

23 BGHZ 180, 134, 141.

24 This question finally becomes relevant, of course, when it comes to claims for damages and compensation: see BGHZ 180, 134, 142.

attributions by others (cf. Luhmann 1995, pp. 82ff., 107ff., 255ff., 313ff.) and that declarations of intent without the willingness to enter into formal contractual relationships[25] hardly deserve the name.

In order to maintain a semblance of preserving the individual assignment of rights and duties, therefore, the extensions of liability are justified with extended duties to examine and safeguard, and various kinds of prognoses concerning imputability and probability are made. This form of attribution of responsibility is almost impossible to calculate and predict, however, especially since it continues to depend to the extent described above on assessments by judges in individual cases (see Peifer 2009; cf. also Hoeren 2008).

The old individualistic concepts are unlikely to provide a way out of the associated legal uncertainty. What is required, therefore, is in the first place a description of social actors and their actions that is adequate to the IT reality and – on this basis – new legal constructions that can meet the challenges of this reality. Only if legal attention focuses more clearly on "living law" – which in this context means, on the inherent rationalities of social communication and information technologies – can the relevant problems in civil and intellectual property law be brought closer to a systematic solution.

2.5 Parts of legal subjects

IT systems can be represented from this perspective as new, artificial components of legal subjects to which correspondingly extended responsibilities are imputed. But they appear to this extent only as dependent parts of subjects, not as partial legal subjects in the sense described at the beginning. They are communicatively coupled with human individuals by virtue of social allocation, so that they form an "association", "assemblage" – in other words, a new socio-technical unity – with the latter.

Evidently, eBay accounts and other IT artifacts can be imputed in such a way that they are already attributed to the sphere of the legal subject, but without need of any other "subjective" self-determinations or volitions on the part of an individual human being. Even if independent or even autonomous actors – wives, children and other family members – become involved and they abuse these artificial extensions to commit legal infringements, that hardly seems to affect the unity of the socio-technical subject of attribution.

25 On the dispensability of the so-called "Erklärungsbewusstsein" see, in particular, BGH NJW 1995, 953; cf. also Habersack 1996, pp. 585; Eisenhardt 1986, pp. 878ff.

The legal subject "human being" originally founded, but also limited, by its psycho-physical integrity and capacity for autonomy is thus extended by a non-human part, namely, IT access via eBay. As part of the extended legal subject, this artifact forthwith gives rise to the extensions of attributions of agency and responsibility described. In this sense it becomes an "agency of changing effectiveness" (Latour 2005, pp. 43ff.; cf. also Schulz-Schaeffer 2008a, p. 706; id. 2008b, pp. 108ff.), which is manifested here specifically as an agency of changes in legal reality. At the same time, the association of human and non-human parts of an extended legal subject also leads people to modify their artificial subject parts, for example, by establishing new technological monitoring options and access restrictions in response to extended imputations of responsibility. But the reciprocal influence exercised by the associated parts alone would not be sufficient to justify speaking of a new socio-technical unit of attribution. Rather, it is the further aspect of the joint constitution of a new, independent actor, of a "hybrid actor" (cf. Schulz-Schaeffer 2008b, pp. 120ff.), that turns the human being-thing association of user and technical access into an extended legal subject.

At the same time, however, the limits of this formation of a unity out of heterogeneous associations should be borne in mind. Not every human-technological interaction inevitably leads to the emergence of new actors. On the contrary, in most cases, it is likely to remain merely a matter of changed role definitions under the reciprocal influence of human being and technology. Only in cases that no longer exhibit any plausible individualizable action responsibilities, but instead involve inseparable human-technological spheres of responsibility, can there be any question of extended legal subjects.

Although it is certainly doubtful in the "Halzband" case whether the association between user and user account should in fact be regarded as inseparable, or whether the numerous possibilities of identity fraud and interventions by third parties do not suggest the contrary, the Federal Court of Justice at any rate assumed such inseparability.[26] As a result, it contrived a legal subject augmented by IT access that can be held responsible both for the consequences of the self-determined, autonomous action of an individual human being as well as for the effects of its associated technological artifacts.[27]

---

26 This inseparability based in particular on the assumed function of the eBay account as "a special means of identification": see BGHZ 180, 134, 139.

27 Therein lies a conceptual similarity to the legal principle of entrepreneurial liability as mentioned above [sections 99 UrhG, 14 (7) MarkenG, 8 (2) UWG]. In the "Halzband" case, however, the association of human individuals and technological artifacts is more than a merely communicative network: As a substantial coupling of users and their

3. Differentiations: Partial Legal Subjectivity in Electronic Commerce

3.1 Information technology actors

With this, a conceivable and in the meantime even commonplace solution option in dealing with recent phenomena of increasingly independent information technologies has already been mapped out. As in cases of the imputation of liability for legal infringements, the concrete expression of will or self-determination on the part of individual human beings could recede into the background also, for example, in the use of software agents and autonomous programs in electronic commerce (cf. Gitter 2007, pp. 29ff., 159ff.). This would pave the way in future for a range of possibilites for no longer imputing electronic declarations of intent in the first instance subjectively, but instead objectively, whether under aspects of prima facie liability (Gitter 2007, p. 180; Oechsler 2008, pp. 568ff.) or in accordance with more abstract risk considerations and prognoses relating to the controllability of the technical procedures (Wiebe 2002, pp. 156ff., 216ff.).

However, the outlook for this kind of imputation, which already seems to be framed especially broadly in the "Halzband" ruling, is poor. Such an extension of the attribution of agency and will through ever broader commercial, examination and security duties, which represent a continuous extension of the human subject of responsibility, will lead sooner or later to excessive demands on human beings as presumptively self-determined individual beings. Put bluntly, the constantly changing imputations of responsibility under information technology law with regard to risk management and threat prevention possibilities become increasingly unreasonable if the responsible subject is supposed to bear ever more liability for third parties through the mediation of information technology.

To be sure, jurisdiction has again limited the implications of "Halzband" liability, for example by not applying its standards to the case of copyright infringement via Wi-Fi[28] and in particular by not applying them to cases involving legal transactions.[29] But – as already indicated – the interests that must be constantly reassessed in ever new single-case trade-offs between "objective" prima facie liability

---

identifying accounts or, more generally, of biological organisms and external resources, it literally forms part of an *information technological incorporation*.

28 Cf. BGHZ 185, 330, 333ff. ("Sommer unseres Lebens"): The IP address of a Wi-Fi connection does not have an identification function comparable to that of eBay accounts.

29 Cf. BGH VersR 2011, 932 = NJW 2011, 2421 (no contractual liability for unauthorized access to an eBay account); for a critical comparison with the "Halzband" decision, see Stadler 2011.

and "subjective" mental elements of the offense are unlikely to make a significant contribution to enhancing legal expectations and certainty.

Instead of determining people's responsibility for their associated IT artifacts in virtually every new constellation via the detour of individual case-based commercial, examination and security duties based on the personal opinions of judges, a systematic solution would have to endeavor to define human and technological spheres of responsibility within clear limits, which deserve general recognition as such with reference to the normative standards observable in electronic commerce.

Then it is quite conceivable – albeit within distinctly narrower limits than those drawn by the "Halzband" ruling – that, for example, the legal acts or violations performed through IT access would be objectively imputed to a correspondingly extended legal subject. This imputation would then be general in nature, however, and would not depend on the breaches of duty and subjective transgressions of the human users that would have to be repeatedly reexamined in individual cases. Those who on this basis are aware from the outset that they are liable in general for a certain part of their IT system can decide for themselves to take additional control and security measures, or to establish a liability fund for possible damages, or also to seek other forms of insurance.

The limits of this imputability of an IT artifact to an extended human-artificial subject are already exceeded, however, in the case of software agents or autonomous programs for generating and transmitting declarations of intent. Software agents and other "autonomous" programs are increasingly turning out to be dynamically operating actors that are likely to count as less and less manageable under risk aspects (cf. Gitter 2007, pp. 174f.; Wiebe 2002, pp. 216ff.). Therefore, they can form at best a loose "human-thing association" with their "agent principals" – an unstable connection that is also continually disrupted by their independent and obstructive behavior. In this regard, a comparison with interpersonal relationships may be much more informative. Could the software agent be more than part of a legal subject after all, perhaps even a partial legal subject?

3.2 Autonomization of partially legally capable actors

When software agents and autonomous programs are used in electronic commerce to conclude contracts, it is almost impossible to attribute their legal behavior to an intention to make a declaration or to perform an action of a concrete human being. Even more so than at the level of liability law, the specific challenge for information technology law is also to grasp the new phenomena of electronic, agent-mediated legal transactions with suitable concepts and to do justice to the associated legal problems by means of corresponding constructions. The central question is: To what extent can such autonomous agents still be attributed to human individuals as their quasi-personal components – and under what conditions do they have to be assigned to other risk spheres, and possibly even be regarded as partially legally capable subjects? (cf. Teubner 2006, pp. 515f.)

Granted, it may already seem unusual enough to regard people and IT systems as associated parts of an extended human-artificial legal subject. Then the idea that the artificial parts could acquire a separate legal subjectivity of their own under certain circumstances may appear even more peculiar. But here one should continue to bear in mind that legal capacity exists in numerous intermediate stages and does not depend directly on any intrinsic properties of an entity, but is instead ascribed on a functional basis.

If software agents no longer operate merely in accordance with predictable programs, but increasingly act in flexible and self-steered ways, if they no longer only operate "automatically" but also in a specific sense "autonomously" – in short, if they act as "autonomous machines" (Gruber/Bung/Ziemann 2014) – why should their legal classification not increasingly fall back on concepts that are already geared to the interventions of independently acting third parties? Consideration should be given especially to the statutory right of representation in German civil law in sections 164ff. BGB, which could also be applied in corresponding ways to software agents as representatives of the human user or "agent principal" (cf. Teubner 2006, pp. 507ff., 520f.).

The application of the rules of representation is generally dismissed out of hand on the grounds that software agents, like other programs, are not autonomously acting legal subjects, and hence are not legally capable, let alone to some limited extent legally competent, and thus lack the preconditions of representation from the beginning (cf., for instance, Cornelius 2002, p. 354f.; Gitter 2007, p. 178; in contrast, fundamental arguments for the personhood of artificial agents are articulated by Solum 1992, pp. 1231ff.; Allen/Widdison 1996, pp. 35ff.; Weitzenböck 2001, pp. 209ff.; Wettig/Zehendner 2004, pp. 122ff.; Andrade *et al.* 2007, pp. 361ff.; Teubner 2006, pp. 505ff.; Sartor 2009, pp. 282ff.). But here it is worth referring once again to Eugen Ehrlich's remarks on legal capacity: there is not just "the" (one) legal capacity. As a social institution, it also exists today – perhaps more than ever – in the plural. Ehrlich already demonstrated emphatically how diverse are the semantic artifacts that we encounter in social and legal communication, whether as more or less limited in their legal capacity or as extended legal subjects, as parts of legal subjects or as partial legal subjects, as persons or as partial persons.

Therefore, it is not at all misconceived to attribute partial legal capacity to software agents and autonomous programs, a legal capacity that is at first limited, to be sure, to the ability to issue legally binding declarations of intent as (quasi-)representatives. In addition, however, they can certainly be conceivably assigned other aspects of legal capacity if need be – for example, the ability to own property – in order to have sufficient recoverable assets available even before a "risk-inclined" use in electronic legal transactions (on the concept of a so-called "electronic Person," see Wettig/Zehendner 2004, pp. 127ff., with further references; on further issues raised by the tortious liability of "intelligent artifacts," cf. Wein 1992, pp. 111ff.). Of course, in this regard other concepts – for example, forms of compulsory insurance modeled on other technological risk domains – must also be considered (cf. Karnow 1996, pp. 193ff.). It can also be conjectured that a right of representation of software agents will develop as a new "special right" in a somewhat different direction from the traditional "human" right of representation (Teubner 2006, pp. 520f.).

3.3 Prospects: Limits of Legal Capacity

In so far as IT systems, on the one hand, and new externalized domains of human personality development, on the other, give rise to new social actors, it might even seem conceivable in principle in the light of what has been said to attribute personality to non-physical, non-living, IT artifacts as well under certain circumstances. However, limitations arise here from the fact that IT systems, in spite of their complexity and communicative capacities, are still not regarded as a general rule as conscious, thinking, perceiving, socially capable beings capable of imitation, let alone as living beings. It must be assumed at any rate that artificial actors will continue to be "personified" in the law differently from living human beings, namely, in ways that correspond to the technological medium.

Here, independent protection of personality and dignity certainly presupposes more than mere legal capacity in the restricted sense envisaged for software agents. It may already be the case that IT systems can no longer be qualified exclusively as purely technical artefacts, but instead simultaneously as social media, and occasionally as independent actors who participate in communication as complex, autonomously operating, possibly even self-willed "agents." They may also be capable of making declarations of intent and of concluding contracts, and should in this respect be considered to be (partially) legal competent. However, this is by no means sufficient to turn them into legally protected entities equipped, for example, with basic rights – not even if they should one day exhibit similarly intelligent behavior to human beings.

Only if artificial entities should succeed in the course of their future development in being integrated into human society as members would recognition of their quasi-personal intrinsic worth also come into consideration. But this presupposes first and foremost a certain social proximity to human beings. If human beings are to adopt a personal stance (fundamentally: Strawson 1962) towards non-human, artificial artifacts, the latter would not only have to act intelligently, but would also have to be perceivable as being similar to human beings. Therefore, they would have to exhibit a certain mental as well as physical identity and, like living creatures, strive for recognition, or at least for attention. Furthermore, they would have to be at least partially socially competent and capable of mutual understanding (cf. Gruber 2006, pp. 119ff.). Only if they fulfill these conditions do they have any prospect of being admitted into human society as beings to whom sympathy and compassion, care and protection, and in particular legal protection of their – to that extent personally grounded – dignity, should be granted.

Personal recognition in human society can be represented accordingly as a "coming-to-the-social-world." It can also be described as a moral and legal birth that presupposes in the first place a social development process in the course of which a being only gradually develops into a member of human society and then ultimately obtains legal personality. The "completion of birth" as a condition of "human legal capacity" (section 1 BGB) is, contrary to appearances, by no means definable in purely empirical terms, but requires first and foremost a normative determination of who belong to the genus "of" human beings and from what point in time their membership in human society is supposed to begin (Gruber 2013). Sufficiently human-like beings, therefore, have a real prospect of one day being treated like human beings, or even of being regarded as human beings.

But similarity to human beings presupposes, in addition to cognitive abilities, also certain bodily features. These can at any rate no longer be considered in isolation from each other. In particular, thinking cannot be reduced, in accordance with older functional, in particular computational, ideas about the human mind, to software and programs that could operate within an in principle arbitrarily configurable hardware (see e.g. Putnam 1960, pp. 148ff.; Block 1995, pp. 377ff.; id. 2007, pp. 27ff. and 141ff.). Rather, thinking is conceivable only on the basis of the "wetware" of a living body (cf. Bray 2009). For a thinking being differs from a merely programmed being precisely in virtue of the fact that its thoughts were not just "programmed into" it by someone else but acquired their meaning through an independent developmental and life history that is the product of autonomous, bodily experience, and as such is authentic.

That in particular also complex cognitive skills can now be understood only as embodied processes is also shown not least by the recent findings in neuroscience on the involvement of the motor nervous system in the neural transformation processes that enable people to locate objects spatially in their environment and perform related movements as actions (Gallese 2005, pp. 23ff.), but also to perceive the actions of other human beings and recognize them as interaction partners (Rizzolatti/Sinigaglia 2008, pp. 79ff.). Therefore, at least human or living bodies are needed that are capable of empathizing, based on their visual and sensorimotor life history, with the actions of their counterparts as though they were actions of their own, and ultimately are able to construct a shared phenomenal space of action through reciprocal observation (cf. Gruber 2012, referring, among others, to Merleau-Ponty 1962).

But this does not rule out that in the distant future an IT system in the bodily form of a more or less humanoid robot might not succeed after all in being regarded as a living being, and even as human-like, despite its artificial origin, because human beings can empathize with its actions like actions of their own and because they perceive it sympathetically as a being with similar experiences, feelings and vulnerabilities – in short, because people feel connected, related, and close to it. However, this would mark the beginning of a new form of legal subjectivity.

References

Allen, Tom, Widdison, Robin (1996): 'Can Computers Make Contracts?', *Harvard Journal of Law & Technology* 9(1), 1996, pp. 25–52.

Andrade, Francisco, Novais, Paulo / Machado, José, Neves, José (2007): "Contracting agents: legal personality and representation." *Artificial Intelligence and Law* 15, pp. 357–373.

Arendt, Hannah (1995): *Elemente und Ursprünge totaler Herrschaft.* Europäische Verlagsanstalt: Frankfurt am Main.

Berberich, Matthias (2010): *Virtuelles Eigentum*, Mohr Siebeck: Tübingen.

Beuthien, Volker (2011): 'Zur Funktion und Verantwortung juristischer Personen im Privatrecht.' *Juristenzeitung* 66(3), pp. 124–130.

Block, Ned (2007): *Consciousness, Function, and Representation.* (Collected Papers Vol. I). MIT Press: Cambridge (Mass.).

Block, Ned (1995): 'The Mind as the Software of the Brain' In: Smith, Edward E., Osherson, Daniel N. Eds., *Thinking. An Invitation to Cognitive Science*, Vol. 3, 2nd ed., MIT Press: Cambridge (Mass.), pp. 377–425.

Bray, Dennis (2009): *Wetware: A Computer in Every Living Cell.* Yale University Press: New Haven.

Bullinger, Winfried, Czychowski, Christian (2011): 'Digitale Inhalte: Werk und/oder Software? Ein Gedankenspiel am Beispiel von Computerspielen' *Gewerblicher Rechtsschutz und Urheberrecht* 113, pp. 19–26.

Cornelius, Kai (2002): 'Vertragsabschluss durch autonome elektronische Agenten' *MultiMedia und Recht* 5(6), pp. 353–358.

Ehrlich, Eugen (1973): *Die Rechtsfähigkeit.* (Reprint of edition published in Berlin, 1909). Scientia: Aalen 1973.

Eisenberg, Jon B. (2008): '*Schiavo* on the Cutting Edge: Functional Brain Imaging and its Impact on Surrogate End-of-Life Decision-Making' *Neuroethics* 1, pp. 75–83.

Eisenhardt, Ulrich (1986): 'Zum subjektiven Tatbestand der Willenserklärung' *Juristenzeitung* 41(19), pp. 875–881.

Esser, Josef (1969): *Wert und Bedeutung der Rechtsfiktionen. Kritisches zur Technik der Gesetzgebung und zur bisherigen Dogmatik des Privatrechts*, 2nd ed., Klostermann: Frankfurt am Main.

Farah, Martha J. (2008): 'Neuroethics and the Problem of Other Minds: Implications of Neuroscience for the Moral Status of Brain-Damaged Patients and Nonhuman Animals' *Neuroethics* 1, pp. 9–18.

Gallese, Vittorio (2005): 'Embodied simulation: From neurons to phenomenal experience' *Phenomenology and the Cognitive Sciences* 4, pp. 23–48.

Gitter, Rotraud (2007): *Softwareagenten im elektronischen Geschäftsverkehr. Rechtliche Vorgaben und Gestaltungsvorschläge.* Nomos: Baden-Baden.

Gruber, Malte-Christian (2013): 'Menschenwürde – Menschlichkeit als Bedingung der Würde?' In: Heike Baranzke, Duttge, Gunnar Eds.: *Würde und Autonomie. Leitprinzipien in Bioethik und Medizinrecht.* Königshausen & Neumann: Würzburg, pp. 417–441.

Gruber, Malte-Christian (2012): 'Normen der Empathie – zur Einfühlung.' In: id., Häußler, Stefan Eds.: *Normen der Empathie.* Trafo: Berlin, pp. 9–20.

Gruber, Malte-Christian (2009): 'Lebenswerk' In: Calliess, Gralf-Peter, Fischer-Lescano, Andreas, Wielsch, Dan, Zumbansen, Peer Eds.: *Soziologische Jurisprudenz. Festschrift für Gunther Teubner zum 65. Geburtstag.* De Gruyter: Berlin, pp. 299–314.

Gruber, Malte-Christian (2006): *Rechtsschutz für nichtmenschliches Leben. Der moralische Status des Lebendigen und seine Implementierung in Tierschutz-, Naturschutz- und Umweltrecht.* Nomos: Baden-Baden.

Gruber, Malte-Christian (2003): 'Vom Kontinuum der Herkunft ins Kontinuum der Zukunft. Zur Relevanz von Argumenten der Potentialität bei der Bestimmung des rechtlichen Status von Biofakten' In: Karafyllis, Nicole Ed.: *Biofakte.*

Versuch über den Menschen zwischen Artefakt und Lebewesen. Mentis: Paderborn, pp. 131–154.

Gruber, Malte-Christian, Bung, Jochen, Ziemann, Sascha (2014) Eds.: *Autonome Automaten. Künstliche Körper und artifizielle Agenten in der technisierten Gesellschaft*. Trafo: Berlin.

Habersack, Mathias (1996): 'Fehlendes Erklärungsbewusstsein mit Wirkung zu Lasten des Erklärungsempfängers?' *Juristische Schulung* 36, pp. 585–588.

Hartmann, Matthias (2011): 'Telemedienrecht' In: Wandtke, Artur-Axel Ed.: *Medienrecht. Praxishandbuch*. Vol. 5, 2nd ed., De Gruyter: Berlin, pp. 1–106.

Hecht, Florian (2009): 'Verantwortlichkeit für Benutzerkonten im Internet' *Kommunikation & Recht* 12(78), pp. 462–465.

Herzog, Otthein *et al.* (2009): *Intelligente Objekte – klein, vernetzt, sensitiv*. Stellungnahme acatech. Deutsche Akademie der Technikwissenschaften): acatech bezieht Position – No. 5, retrieved 12.11.2014, from http://www.acatech.de/fileadmin/user_upload/Baumstruktur_nach_Website/Acatech/root/de/Publikationen/Stellungnahmen/acatech_bezieht_Position_intelligente_Objekte_web.pdf

Hoeren, Thomas (2008): 'Das Pferd frisst keinen Gurkensalat – Überlegungen zur Internet Governance' *Neue Juristische Wochenschrift* 61(36), pp. 2615–2619.

Jhering, Rudolf von (1857): 'Unsere Aufgabe' *Jherings Jahrbücher* 1, pp. 1–52.

Kant, Immanuel (1996): *The Metaphysics of Morals* Ed. and trans. Mary Gregor). Cambridge University Press: Cambridge.

Karnow, Curtis E. A. (1996): 'Liability for Distributed Artificial Intelligences' *Berkeley Technology Law Journal* 11(1), pp. 147–204.

Krebs, Peter, Becker, Maximilian (2009): 'Die Teilverdinglichung und ihre Anwendung auf Internetdomains' *Juristenzeitung* 64(19), pp. 932–943.

Latour, Bruno: *Reassembling the Social. An Introduction to Actor-Network-Theory*. Oxford University Press: Oxford / New York 2005.

Latour, Bruno (1993): *We Have Never Been Modern*. (Trans. Catherine Porter). Harvard University Press: Cambridge (Mass.).

Leistner, Matthias: "Störerhaftung und mittelbare Schutzrechtsverletzung." *Gewerblicher Rechtsschutz und Urheberrecht – Beilage* 112, 2010, pp. 1–32.

Luhmann, Niklas (1995): *Social Systems*. (Trans. John Bednarz with Dirk Baecker). Stanford University Press: Stanford.

Merleau-Ponty, Maurice: *Phenomenology of Perception*. (Trans. Colin Smith). Routledge & Kegan Paul: London 1962.

Müller, Sabine (2010): 'Revival der Hirntod-Debatte: Funktionelle Bildgebung für die Hirntod-Diagnostik' *Ethik in der Medizin* 22, pp. 5–17.

Oechsler, Jürgen: 'Die Bedeutung des § 172 Abs. 1 BGB beim Handeln unter fremdem Namen im Internet' *Archiv für die civilistische Praxis* 208, pp. 565–583.

Peifer, Karl-Nikolaus (2009): 'Verkehrspflicht des Nutzers einer Auktionsplattform zur Geheimhaltung der elektronischen Zugangsdaten ('Halzband')' *JurisPR-WettbR* (5), comment 1.

Putnam, Hilary (1960): 'Minds and Machines' In: Hook, Sidney Ed.: *Dimensions of Mind. A Symposium*, New York University Press: New York, pp. 148–179.

Raiser, Thomas (1999): 'Der Begriff der juristischen Person. Eine Neubesinnung' *Archiv für die civilistische Praxis* 199, pp. 104–144.

Renzikowski, Joachim (1997): *Restriktiver Täterbegriff und fahrlässige Beteiligung*. Mohr Siebeck: Tübingen .

Reuter, Dieter (2007): 'Rechtsfähigkeit und Rechtspersönlichkeit. Rechtstheoretische und rechtspraktische Anmerkungen zu einem großen Thema.' *Archiv für die civilistische Praxis* 207, pp. 673–717.

Rizzolatti, Giacomo, Sinigaglia, Corrado (2008): *Mirrors in the Brain: How Our Minds Share Actions and Emotions*. Oxford University Press: Oxford.

Rössel, Markus (2009): 'Anmerkung' (Comment on BGH, Urteil vom 11.03.2009 – I ZR 114/06). *Computer und Recht* 25, pp. 453–455.

Roßler, Gustav (2008): 'Kleine Galerie neuer Dingbegriffe: Hybriden, Quasi-Objekte, Grenzobjekte, epistemische Dinge' In: Kneer, Georg, Schroer, Markus, Schüttpelz, Erhard Eds.: *Bruno Latours Kollektive. Kontroversen zur Entgrenzung des Sozialen*. Suhrkamp: Frankfurt am Main, pp. 76–107.

Sartor, Giovanni (2009): 'Cognitive automata and the law: electronic contracting and the intentionality of software agents' *Artificial Intelligence and Law* 17, pp. 253–290.

Savigny, Friedrich Carl von (1840): *System des heutigen römischen Rechts* II. Veit: Berlin.

Schulz-Schaeffer, Ingo (2008a): 'Technik als sozialer Akteur und als soziale Institution. Sozialität von Technik statt Postsozialität' In: Rehberg, Karl-Siegbert Ed: *Die Natur der Gesellschaft.* (Verhandlungen des 33. Kongresses der Deutschen Gesellschaft für Soziologie in Kassel 2006). Campus: Frankfurt am Main, pp. 703–719.

Schulz-Schaeffer, Ingo (2008b): 'Technik in heterogener Assoziation. Vier Konzepte der gesellschaftlichen Wirklichkeit von Technik im Werk Latours.' In: Kneer, Georg, Schroer, Markus, Schüttpelz, Erhard Eds.: *Bruno Latours Kollektive. Kontroversen zur Entgrenzung des Sozialen*. Suhrkamp: Frankfurt am Main, pp. 108–152.

Solum, Lawrence B. (1992): 'Legal Personhood for Artificial Intelligences' *North Carolina Law Review* 70(4), pp. 1231–1287.

Spindler, Gerald (2011a): 'Der Schutz virtueller Gegenstände' *Zeitschrift für Geistiges Eigentum / Intellectual Property Journal* 3, pp. 129–150.

Spindler, Gerald (2011b): 'Präzisierungen der Störerhaftung im Internet. Besprechung des BGH-Urteils 'Kinderhochstühle im Internet', *Gewerblicher Rechtsschutz und Urheberrecht* 113, pp. 101–108.

Stadler, Thomas (2011): 'Keine vertragliche Haftung bei missbräuchlicher Nutzung eines eBay-Accounts' *JurisPR-ITR* (14), comment 2.

Strawson, Peter F. (1962): 'Freedom and resentment' *Proceedings of the British Academy* 48, pp. 1–25.

Teubner, Gunther (2006): 'Rights of Non-humans? Electronic Agents and Animals as New Actors in Politics and Law' *Journal of Law and Society* 33(4), pp. 497–521.

Teubner, Gunther (1987): 'Unternehmenskorporatismus. New Industrial Policy und das 'Wesen' der Juristischen Person' *Kritische Vierteljahresschrift für Gesetzgebung und Rechtswissenschaft* 2, pp. 61–85.

Ulsenheimer, Klaus (2007): 'Hirntod und Intensivmedizin. Juristische Probleme.' *Der Anaesthesist* 58, pp. 722–727.

Ungern-Sternberg, Joachim von (2010): 'Die Rechtsprechung des Bundesgerichtshofs zum Urheberrecht und zu den verwandten Schutzrechten in den Jahren 2008 und 2009 (Teil II)'. *Gewerblicher Rechtsschutz und Urheberrecht* 112, pp. 386–396..

Varelius, Jukka (2009): 'Minimally Conscious State and Human Dignity'. *Neuroethics* 2, pp. 35–50.

Vesting, Thomas (2003): 'Das Internet und die Notwendigkeit der Transformation des Datenschutzes' In: Ladeur, Karl-Heinz Ed.: *Innovationsoffene Regulierung des Internet. Neues Recht für Kommunikationsnetzwerke.* Nomos: Baden-Baden, pp. 155–190.

Wein, Leon E. (1992): 'The Responsibility of Intelligent Artifacts: Toward an Automation Jurisprudence' *Harvard Journal of Law & Technology* 6(1), pp. 103–154.

Weitzenböck, Emily M. (2001): 'Electronic Agents and the Formation of Contracts' *International Journal of Law and Information Technology* 9(3), pp. 204–234.

Wettig, Steffen, Zehendner, Eberhard (2004): 'A legal analysis of human and electronic agents' *Artificial Intelligence and Law* 12, pp. 111–135.

Wiebe, Andreas (2002): *Die elektronische Willenserklärung. Kommunikationstheoretische und rechtsdogmatische Grundlagen des elektronischen Geschäftsverkehrs.* Mohr Siebeck: Tübingen.

Wiethölter, Rudolf (1992): 'Zur Regelbildung in der Dogmatik des Zivilrechts' In: Herberger, Maximilian, Neumann, Ulfrid, Rüßmann, Helmut Eds.: *Generalisierung und Individualisierung im Rechtsdenken.* Steiner: Stuttgart, pp. 222–240.

Miodrag Jovanović

Constructing Legal Personality of Collective Entities – The Case of "Peasants"

1. Introduction

When Christopher Stone in 1972 made a revolutionary case in favor of legal rights for natural objects, such as trees, he noticed that "[t]hroughout legal history, each successive extension of rights to some new entity has been [...] a bit unthinkable." This is so, because "[w]e are inclined to suppose the rightlessness of rightless 'things' to be a decree of Nature, not a legal convention acting in support of sonic status quo." (Stone 2010 p. 2)

The very idea of vesting rights in collective entities was met with a similar reluctance, particularly within the camp of liberal political philosophers. However, as Narveson put it, collective rights talk is not nonsensical, because, otherwise, "there would be no normative question" behind it. If one, for instance, asserts – "It makes no sense to talk of collective rights; therefore we should not recognize any" – then one has to explain "what is it whose *recognition* we should not engage in". Hence, it is possible to understand the claim that collectives have rights, just as it is possible to understand the claim that rocks have rights. Narveson concludes that precisely because these statements are comprehensible, "we can understand the inimical implications of such theses, and should reject them." This rejection can be taken only in the form of a normative argument, and this is exactly what Narveson does by defending "a kind of 'individualism'". (Narveson, 1991, p. 329)

2. Legal Personality and Moral Standing

The entire legal history testifies to the fact that overcoming status quo and dominant legal conventions has always required fostering a normative-moral argument in favor of the right-holding capacity of a certain being or entity.[1] The notorious racial doctrine, for example, was premised on the idea that part of humanity was

1 One may argue, and rightly so, that moral standing was not the key precondition for the recognition of legal personhood of corporate entities. This by no means implies that the legal status of these entities cannot be addressed in moral terms. Take, for example, the ongoing debate on "corporate social responsibility". *See, e.g.*, Bassen, Jastram, Meyer, 2005, pp. 231–236.

destined to be excluded from the status of legal subjects in virtue of its skin color, which was only a sign of its moral inferiority. Take the following statement of the infamous *Dred Scott* decision of the US Supreme Court. In commenting the "all men are born equal" phrase of the Declaration of Independence, the Court's majority states that the drafters perfectly understood the meaning of the language they used [...] and they knew that it would not in any part of the civilized world be supposed to embrace the negro race, which by common consent, had been excluded from civilized Governments and the family of nations, and doomed to slavery.[2]

Consequently, the normative-moral standpoint of substantial equality of human beings needed to prevail before we could solemnly proclaim in Article 6 of the *Universal Declaration of Human Rights* that "[e]veryone has the right to recognition everywhere as a person before the law."

The same applies to the claim that animals can possess rights. Jeremy Bentham was aware that his proposition of the equal moral worth of human and animal species was far ahead of moral convictions of his time, when famously uttered:

> The day may come when the rest of the animal creation may acquire those rights which never could have been withholden from them but by the hand of tyranny. The French have already discovered that the blackness of the skin is no reason why a human being should be abandoned without redress to the caprice of a tormentor [...] A full-grown horse or dog is beyond comparison a more rational, as well as a more conversable animal, than an infant of a day, or a week, or even month, old. But suppose the case were otherwise, what would it avail? The question is not, Can they *reason?* nor, Can they *talk?* but, Can they *suffer?* (Bentham, 1988, pp. 310–311)

What seemed highly unlikely then, or even half a century ago, has now become a legitimate topic of discussion of both political philosophers and legal scholars.[3] In some legal systems, animals are a step from the recognition of a full-fledged legal personhood. Take, for example, the provision of Section 90a of the German Civil Code (Burgerliches Gesetzbuch (BGB)), which states: "Animals are not things. They are protected by special statutes. They are governed by the provisions that apply to things, with the necessary modifications, except insofar as otherwise provided."[4]

Jones is, thus, right in claiming that the question of whether legal personality can be extended to collective entities also "turns upon the attribution of moral

---

2 *Dred Scott v. Sanford*, 60 U.S. 393 (1857).

3 *See, e.g.*, Sunstein, Nussbaum, 2004; Donaldson, Kymlicka, 2011).

4 BGB, English translation at http://www.gesetze-im-internet.de/englisch_bgb/englisch_bgb.html.

standing." Simply put, "someone or something can hold rights only if it is the sort of thing to which duties can be owed and which is capable of being wronged." That is, "moral standing is a precondition of right-holding." (Jones, 1999, pp. 361–362)

Now, various legal instruments, at both domestic and international level, have for a long time operated with formulations that give rise to the claim that groups can qualify for the status of right-holders.[5] However, in the presence of the dominant convention that rights can be vested only in natural and juristic persons, substantial doubts remained as to whether this claim was warranted. I argued elsewhere in more detail that the case in favor of collectives as right-holders can be made and that the present legal practice can be rendered more intelligible if collective rights are treated as grounded in the normative-moral standpoint of *value collectivism*. (Jovanović, 2012) This is a philosophical view, according to which "a collective entity can have value independently of its contribution to the well-being of individual human beings." (Hartney, 1991, p. 297)

Let me briefly summarize the argument in favor of value collectivism. This stance implies, first, that collectives can be said to exist somehow independently from its members. Take the crime of genocide. It is premised on the idea that the group physical existence can be detached from the existence of its individual members, not necessarily in phenomenological terms, but in terms of a conceptually distinctive *good* worthy of criminal protection. Consequently, the criminalized "intent to destroy, in whole or in part" relevant groups can, in principle, be established even if the killing involved a single group member, provided that it was directed at the group "as such".[6] This leads to the second thesis of value collectivism, namely, that collectives can have own genuine interests that are not mere aggregation of individual interests of group members. This thesis implies that it must be possible, conceptually speaking, for collective interest "to conflict with the interest of *most* of the members of the group." (Hartney, p. 300) But, again, this need not be difficult to demonstrate. Few, for example, would be ready to argue that German nation would not be better off without Nazis in power, even though most of Germans of that time thought that this regime was in their best interest. This takes us to the final thesis of value collectivism, according to which collective interests can be inherently valuable, that is, their moral importance does not

---

5 As early as 1970s, Van Dyke noticed that "group identified by race, language, or religion have rights", which "creates a problem in theory and philosophy as well as in law." Van Dyke, 1974, p. 740.

6 To be sure, establishing the genocidal intent on a single murder case would in practice be extremely difficult, if not impossible task for a prosecutor. For a meticulous analysis of all the constitutive elements of the crime of genocide, *see* May, 2010.

depend on them contributing to the well-being of individual group members. One of the most often employed refutations of this thesis rests on the argument of "the truth of value-individualism" (Hartney, p. 298)[7], which, in return, implies that the contrary standpoint is "counterintuitive". (Boshammer, p. 134)

To this one can respond by reminding that there is nothing self-evidently true in value individualism, insofar as it is a product of one historical era, which in certain respects may very well be behind us. To state that we live in times in which the group interest to self-preservation and flourishing is often taken as value in itself is not necessarily to express an evaluative statement, but simply to acknowledge that value collectivism is, after all, not so counterintuitive as suggested by the opposite camp. Recognized collective rights are ultimately grounded in those vital and inherent collective interests. The most important implication of *value collectivism* is that collective rights can at times override individual rights of group members.[8]

3. Legal Drafting of the Personality of Collective Entities

After providing a brief general account of moral standing of collective entities, which justifies their recognition as an independent category of legal right-holders, different from natural and juristic persons, I move to the question of how to draft legal personality of collective entities. Legal drafting, in this respect, should not be confused with the jurisprudential task of constructing the concept of collective rights.[9] Whereas jurisprudence provides some general criteria regarding the necessary conditions under which the status of legal subject may be acquired or lost, it is upon legal practice to determine more precise requirements, as well as exceptions and variations within respective legal systems. One may argue that this is a political question that falls completely within the competence of legal drafting

7 Boshammer also argues that "the claim of the prime importance of individual's freedom and well-being worthy of protection against any collective aims and collective 'entities' has reached the status of an objective truth", insofar as "nobody in the western world and in occidental philosophy doubts the claim seriously and hence it can be taken for certain." Boshammer, 2003, p. 137.

8 Most of the authors defending the standpoint of *value individualism*, according to which collective entities can have only instrumental and not the inherent value, end up allowing the possibility that collective rights sometimes outweigh individual group members' rights. Cf. Buchanan, Allen: "Liberalism and Group Rights". In: Coleman, 1994, pp. 1–15; Kymlicka, 1995, pp. 43–44. This outcome, however, is tenable only when grounding collective rights in the rival standpoint of *value collectivism*.

9 See in more detail, Jovanović, Ch. 3.

authorities.[10] I will, however, try to show that legal theory is capable of providing some useful general methodological guidelines. It will do so by answering, for instance, the following questions: what general principles should be followed in transforming the pre-given, social identity of group into the legal personality; what in the language of legal drafting of collective personality might positively/negatively affect the subsequent processes of legal interpretation and adjudication; what techniques of legal drafting are the most adequate for the purpose of protecting certain collective interests and goods, etc.

It is important to stress that there is a thin, yet distinguishable, line between the methodological tasks of legal theory and legal practice. Legal theorists are in the business of conceptualizing legal personality of collective entities, based on both commendable and deplorable instances of legal practice, while legal practice is faced with the task of putting in the operative use the general right-holding capacity of collectives, by granting them legal status within the given legal system. There are potential mutually reinforcing benefits for both branches. On the one hand, in its treatment of collectives as right-holders, legal practice will have jurisprudential resources of general methodological guidelines to follow (and it is free in deciding whether to do so). On the other hand, jurisprudence will have a wealth of experience to reflect upon and, if necessary, to reconstruct the general concept of collectives as right-holders (and the demands of scientific rigor will obviously oblige theory to do so). When aforementioned methodological guidelines for the legal drafting process are discussed in more detail, it becomes obvious why jurisprudence can perform this task only by relying on the assistance of social sciences, such as sociology and anthropology. This is so due to the fact that jurisprudence finds itself in a peculiar situation of dealing with an emerging concept. To top it all off, one of the distinctive features of the putative right-holder is its largely constituted social identity that has to be given the form of legal personality.

3.1 Heinze's scheme of the "construction of difference"

Let me start by discussing the process of legal recognition of the separate legal personality of a certain group. The underlying normative assumption of the collective rights talk concerns the recognition of uniqueness of the group

10 This argument, for instance, is often employed in German debates on legal methodology. According to the argument, jurists have nothing there to deal with. However, as pointed out by Bydlinski, this radical thesis can be rejected on the basis of a simple historical fact that jurists were and will be always involved in the law drafting process (*Gesetzgebung*). (Bydlinski, 1982, p. 621)

particularity, as opposed to the universality of "sameness".[11] Consequently, drafting a legal norm that will vest rights in a certain group is necessarily taken in the form of legal recognition of that group's social distinctiveness. At this point, jurisprudence can benefit from some conceptual schemes developed in social sciences, in particular, from Eric Heinze's work on the "minority" concept. According to him, the process of "the construction of difference" consists of three steps. The first one is "recognition of other peoples or groups as such – as different from one's own, on the basis of, e.g., kinship, geography, language, anatomy, religion or customs." The second step "consists of naming the difference", while the third one concerns "evaluation of that difference through attribution of normative significance to it." (Heinze, 1999, p. 34.)

This last step can be further sub-divided, as the normative conclusions correlate the other two steps – "One normative correlate is supremacism, another is egalitarianism." (Heinze, p. 35) Finally, the latter normative stance can take either the form of "universalist egalitarianism" (as in the *Universal Declaration of Human Rights*) or "differentialist egalitarianism" (as, for instance, in *Convention concerning Indigenous and Tribal Peoples in Independent Countries*). While in the former case "equality" is "construed to mean that no differences among peoples would justify different treatment", in the latter case, it is "construed to mean that differences are worthwhile, and can and should be maintained on equal footing". (Heinze, p. 36)

As for the step of social naming and labeling, legal drafters, as a rule, should follow the social attribution that is accepted by the group in question, because it will potentially enhance the prospects for the wider and smoother applicability of the legal rule. Legal practice, however, provides examples of disregard for this general methodological principle of legal drafting. Indicative in that respect is the German policy of creating *Ausländerbeirate* (foreigners' councils), as consultative bodies of local governments, which represent interest of immigrant communities. In criticizing this solution, Offe notices:

> People represented by such councils often belong to half a dozen or more different nationalities. It would never occur to them having their identity cast in terms of being "foreigners", an identity label that is entirely shaped by the perceptions and preferences of the domestic majority population. (Offe, 1998, n. 26)

Sometimes, however, members of the given group eventually accept this sort of artificial exogenous group categorization. Take, for instance, the case of the

---

11 This is the reason why harsh liberals accuse "the politics of recognition" of being an "anti-Enlightenment" politics that purports to destroy universalism, *see, e.g.*, Berry, 2001.

American Indians, who for a long time remained faithful to their own separate tribal self-identification, but after decades of a uniform social and administrative treatment, they largely accepted this imposed overarching identity.[12]

3.2 Which groups qualify?

Heinze's schema has a "heuristic" function, which means that this three-step process "purports only to reconstruct three defining 'moments' – albeit not in a strictly temporal sense – that can be discerned". As a result, these three steps are sometimes hardly distinguishable in social reality. What general methodological principles can jurisprudence formulate and offer to legal drafters in regard to the problem of groups qualifying for the status of right-holder? For one, just as it is patently clear that not all socially identifiable markers of group belonging would be equally relevant for the outsiders' perception and recognition of separate group existence in sociological terms, so it is obvious that legal recognition can be extended to a much smaller number of socially recognized groups. It is incumbent upon jurisprudence to determine some general formal qualities that groups have to meet as a precondition for the right-holding capacity, as well as to offer to legal drafters a non-exhaustive list of groups that normally qualify for this status. The most legal theory can formulate in abstract terms is that these qualities have roughly to match the features that drafters of the Genocide Convention had in mind when discussing which groups qualify for protection. What they particularly had in mind was that the groups in question should be "distinct", "permanent", "stable", "sharing a common origin" or having "characteristic features in common", the membership in them should not be "optional", but "inevitable", they could be identified by "objective criteria".[13] These groups obviously play a "constitutive role"

---

12 As pointed out by Mitnick, "the social label 'American Indian' reveals more about the European explorers' true original objective (i.e. to locate a trade route to the East Indies), than it does about the ethnically diverse population to whom the label became attached." Mitnick, 2006, p. 76.

13 There was a great deal of debate whether religious groups could be included in light of one's freedom to join or leave a religious group. In spite of this, they stayed within the circle of protected groups. On the other hand, political groups were disqualified on account of not being stable enough, whereas economic groups were found not to be clearly defined. Thornberry, however, rightly points out that "if stability is a key for inclusion of a group, the omission of linguistic groups is surprising, because such groups could claim to be as 'stable' and 'permanent', as, for example, national or religious groups". Thornberry, 1991, p. 68.

in the life of their members, in terms of the adopted values and life perspectives. (Boshammer, p. 85)

Most importantly, "they simply are given for members and non-members alike, by the signs used and identified, by mutual recognition paid by members to each other, and by regard of outsiders". (Kis, 1996, p. 221.) This, finally, means that, unlike juristic persons, "they are not the creatures of law or the state". (Van Dyke, Oxford 1995, p. 33.) Put this way, the best jurisprudence can come with is the thesis that "traditional" constitutive groups – such as those recognized in international law as peoples, minorities, and indigenous peoples – seem to be more obvious candidates for holding rights than some other social groups.

3.3 Legal definition of group membership

One of the issues that legal drafters of collective personality have to take into account, because of its potential influence on the processes of legal interpretation and adjudication, concerns the legal definition of group membership. Normally, adjudicators will have to rely on the pre-legal, social criteria of group membership in order to decide whether the given legal norm applies in the particular case. This is, actually, one of the defining features of collectives as right-holders, which differentiates them from juristic persons. However, legal practice provides plenty of contrary examples, where legislators intend to provide precise definitions of group membership. Some of these examples are notorious, because they represent instances of legally institutionalized supremacism of one group over another. Take the Nazi Nurnberg Race Laws, which tried to determine who was to count as a "full Jew". Eventually, this category was ascribed to a person with at least three Jewish grandparents. Those with less were designated as *Mischlinge* (the Germans of mixed race) of two degrees: the first degree – with two Jewish grandparents; the second degree – with one Jewish grandparent.[14] Similar legislative efforts can be found at the beginning of 20th century in the southern states of the USA. Their intent was to implement the so-called "one drop rule" in determining the category of "whites". One of the "Jim Crow laws" is the State of Virginia's 1924 act on racial integrity, which *inter alia* states:

> For the purpose of this act, the term "white person" shall apply only to the person who has no trace whatsoever of any blood other than Caucasian; but persons who have

14 English version of Nurnberg laws is available in: Noakes, Pridham, 1974, pp. 463–467.

> one-sixteenth or less of the blood of the American Indian and have no other non-Caucasic blood shall be deemed to be white persons.[15]

This infamous legacy implies one of the general methodological guidelines for legal drafters when recognizing collective entities as legal subjects. They should not try to achieve "legal determinacy" by using the language of "hard" factors, for this attempt may easily end up in something resembling the Nazi-like "legal eugenics". For one thing, even in other less intricate areas of life, the legal drafting ideal of full determinacy through "precise" language formulations and criteria is hardly attainable, and will not necessarily prevent "hard cases" of interpretation and adjudication.[16] Consequently, if legal drafters are to avoid dangerous sideways of "legal eugenics", they need to operate more flexibly with categories of collective social identities.

It is already indicated that legal drafting authorities are politically free to accept or reject general methodological guidelines of jurisprudence.[17] However, in case jurisprudential project of conceptualizing collective rights and collectives as a third category of right-holders succeeds, this will help overcoming the current phase of treating collectives as "unacknowledged presence".[18] Such a development in jurisprudence will, finally, mean that if international and municipal instruments' explicit or implicit purpose is to provide protection for certain groups, then legal drafters would have stronger reasons to abandon now dominant "persons-belonging-to" formula, which leaves doubt as to whether rights in question are individual or collective. The present *nomotechnique* was largely driven by the

---

15 *An Act to Preserve Racial Integrity* (1924), available at www.eugenicsarchive.org/html/eugenics/index2.html?tag=1239.

16 See, in general, Bix, 1993.

17 Apart from these specific guidelines, legal drafters should also follow some more general principles established by jurisprudence. Bydlinski speaks of several such principles: 1. the principle of economy, which means that certain regulation should be drafted in as less legal rules as possible (this principle consists of the following sub-principles of a) generality, instead of casuistic; b) reduction; and c) cross-referencing); 2. the principle of adequacy, comprehensibility and, depending on the circumstances, precision of legal expressions; 3. the principle of the systematical and coherent order of the presentation of legal material (*Rechtsstoff*); and 4. the principle of adequate announcement. (Bydlinski, pp. 625–626).

18 In the concluding part of his book on minority rights, Thornberry says that, presently, "the group is 'unacknowledged presence' behind the individual rights. Collective rights are a substantive, if not a 'formal' aspect of legal entity." This leads him to conclude that "'[m]inority rights' are substantive and indirect, not formal and direct." (Thornberry, 1991, p. 396).

general post-Second World War political trend of avoiding the League of Nations' collective protection rhetoric. One of the tasks of a legal theory of collective rights is to provide clear criteria for a more precise classification of collective and individual rights, which will then serve as a reliable methodological guideline for the process of legal drafting. This guideline would eventually point to the use of linguistic techniques that directly vest rights in collective entities, instead of the members of the group.

4. "Peasants" as Holders of Collective Rights?

Probably the most controversial issue regarding the jurisprudential project of conceptualizing collectives as a different category of right-holders concerns the question of potential candidates for such status. The preceding analysis demonstrates that, based on the relevant legal practice, jurisprudence can come up only with a non-exhaustive list of formal qualities that putative collective right-holders have to possess, which eventually puts certain "traditional" groups, such as peoples, minorities and indigenous peoples, in a favorable position. However, throughout the world there are different social movements that express their claims by using the rhetoric of collective rights. One of them is the agrarian movement Via Campesina, which in its more than two decades long struggle for a better position of peasants and other people working in rural areas managed to draw attention of both national governments and the United Nations' bodies.[19] Most notably, after the movement's adoption of its own *Declaration on the Rights of Peasants – Women and Men* in 2008,[20] the UN Human Rights Council tasked its Advisory Committee to propose ways and means to further protect the rights of these categories. The Advisory Committee presented its final study in 2012, with a draft Declaration in Annex.[21] Eventually, an open-ended intergovernmental working group was formed with the task of elaborating a UN Declaration on the rights of peasants and other people working in rural areas.[22]

Even though "[r]ights occupy a central place in most Via Campina statements" (Claeys, 2013), one is able to notice that the movement is somewhat simultaneously fostering claims for both "the *right of peoples to food sovereignty*,

---

19 http://viacampesina.org/en/.

20 Available at: http://viacampesina.net/downloads/PDF/EN-3.pdf.

21 Final study of the Human Rights Council Advisory Committee on the advancement of the rights of peasants and other people working in rural areas, A/HRC/19/75, 24 February 2012.

22 For a brief history of the creation of this working group, *see*, Golay, 2013.

which insists on distributional claims", as well as "the *rights of peasants* [which] emphasize questions of recognition." (Claeys 2013, p. 8) There is an obvious tension between these two sorts of claims, because they are supposed to respond to different types of conflicts. Whereas *interest*-based conflicts are over resources, and the means for coping with them are social rights, the *identity*-based conflicts are over group recognition and respect, and their "antidote" is group (collective) rights. (Offe, pp. 121–123)[23] Accordingly, Claeys is correct in stressing "distinct trajectories" of these two rights-claims. The former "requires a total revamp of global governance of trade in agriculture and constitutes a direct opposition to the (inimical) WTO framework", while the latter "requires that the (inoffensive) UN human rights system acknowledge the existence of a new group right." (Claeys, 2012, p. 854)

The right to food sovereignty is a novel theoretical construct that has the collectivist overtone, but in all countries in which it found its way into constitutional instruments, such as Venezuela, Ecuador, Mali and Bolivia, it is "directly tied to the industrialization of agriculture and agrofuels, the rising cost of fertilizer, free trade policies, and the privatization of resources."[24] Hence, it is normally framed in the language of state responsibility to develop certain set of economic and social policies pertaining to sustainable food production and the development of rural areas.[25] Although peoples and other groups, such as "communities, pueblos and nationalities" in Article 281 of the Constitution of Ecuador, are designated as direct beneficiaries of the food sovereignty, it is clear from the nature of the stated structural economic measures and policies that, even if they can be institutionalized in the form of concomitant rights, most rights in question would be individual in nature.[26]

---

23 I take both phrases – "group rights" and "collective rights" – to denote one and the same thing, that a right is vested in a certain group (collective).

24 Beauregard, 2009, p. 46.

25 Take, for example, Article 404 of Bolivian constitution, which states as follows: "Integrated sustainable rural development is a fundamental part of the economic policies of the State, which gives priority to efforts to promote of common economic undertakings and the assembly of rural people, with emphasis on security and on food sovereignty..." Quoted from: Beauregard, 2009, p. 56.

26 Take, for instance, the following State commitments envisaged by the aforementioned article of the Constitution of Ecuador: "to promote small and medium sized production and the social economies of the food and fishery industries; adopt fiscal policies, tributaries, and tariffs to protect the food and fishery sectors against dependency on foreign food imports; strengthen diversification and introduce ecological and organic technologies into agriculture; promote redistributive policies and access to productive

In contrast, both Via Campesina's 2008 Declaration and the Advisory Board's Draft Declaration put emphasis on peasants' rights.[27] In order to that, they proceed from a detailed, and rather extensive, definition of "peasants":

1. A peasant is a man or woman of the land, who has a direct and special relationship with the land and nature through the production of food or other agricultural products. Peasants work the land themselves and rely above all on family labour and other small-scale forms of organizing labour. Peasants are traditionally embedded in their local communities and they take care of local landscapes and of agro-ecological systems.
2. The term peasant can apply to any person engaged in agriculture, cattle-raising, pastoralism, handicrafts related to agriculture or a similar occupation in a rural area. This includes indigenous people working on the land.
3. The term peasant also applies to the landless. According to the Food and Agriculture Organization of the United Nations definition, the following categories of people are considered to be landless and are likely to face difficulties in ensuring their livelihood:

   (a) Agricultural labour households with little or no land;
   (b) Non-agricultural households in rural areas, with little or no land, whose members are engaged in various activities such as fishing, making crafts for the local market, or providing services;
   (c) Other rural households of pastoralists, nomads, peasants practising shifting cultivation, hunters and gatherers, and people with similar livelihoods.

---

resources such as land and water; establish financial support systems for small and medium producers; promote rehabilitation and preservation of agro-biodiversity, ancestral knowledge, and seed exchange; guarantee the health of animals for human consumption; ensure the development of scientific investigations and innovative technologies that are appropriate for food sovereignty; regulate the use and development of biotechnology through bio-security standards; strengthen the development of producer and consumer organizations and networks and the commercialization and distribution of food to promote equality in rural and urban areas; generate just systems of distribution and commercialization of food, decrease the monopolization and speculation of food; provide food to victims of natural disasters without monopolistic practices or speculation; prevent consumption of contaminated food; purchase food and materials for social programs primarily for networks of small producers." Quoted from: Beauregard, p. 48.

27 Hence, the Draft Declaration states that this instrument "is an essential step towards the recognition, promotion and protection of the rights of peasants".

The subsequent provision of Article 2 of both instruments deals in general with the nature and the holder of rights belonging to peasants. This provision, first, stresses inter-gender equality of members of peasants' community; second, it contains the clause on prohibition of their discrimination, particularly on social, economic, or cultural grounds; finally, it guarantees to peasants the enjoyment of all the internationally protected human rights. It is this last element of the provision which raises doubts with respect to the nature of rights in question, as well as to the identity of right-holder. Whereas the Via Campesina Declaration states that "[p]easants (women and men) have the right to the full enjoyment [of international human rights], *as a collective or as individuals*", the Advisory Board's Draft Declaration speaks of peasants having the right to fully enjoy international human rights "*individually and collectively*". Hence, the former provision might implicate that some rights are held by peasants "as a collective", while the latter implies that some human rights can be exercised "collectively". Do these normative statements amount to the same claim? That is, are some international human rights collective in virtue of the fact that they are exercised collectively?

The identification of collectively exercised individual rights and collective rights is one of the most often made mistakes in the debate. The peasants' rights discussion is no exception in this respect. For instance, in his background paper, prepared for the first session of the working group on the rights of peasants and other people working in rural areas, Golay notices that some states expressed their concern about recognizing collective rights of peasants. Yet, in his opinion, "this reluctance might be misplaced", because "an analysis of the human rights instruments adopted in the last 40 years demonstrates that, with few exceptions, all human rights can be described as individual rights that can be exercised collectively." (Golay, p. 16) This view is, however, rejected in the Explanatory Report of the Council of Europe's *Framework Convention for the Protection of National Minorities*, which explicitly states that the possibility of joint exercise of certain guaranteed rights and freedoms "is distinct from the notion of collective rights".[28] Collective rights are rights vested in groups *qua* groups for the protection of their inherent, non-reducible interests and, just like individual rights,[29] they can be exercised in either of the three following ways: collectively (e.g. the right of a people to self-determination); by a representative body (e.g. the right of a minority

28 *Framework Convention for the Protection of National Minorities – Explanatory Report*, ETS no. 157, par. 37.

29 The typical example of individual rights which can be exercised only jointly are freedoms of association and assembly.

to represent its culture in national cultural institutions); individually, by a group member (e.g. the right of an indigenous people to fishery).[30]

In order to speak of peasants' collective rights, one need, first, to elucidate the nature of rights in question, and second, to determine whether "peasants" qualify for the status of the collective right-holder. These two requirements are intricately connected, though. As stated, collective rights are those generated by genuine collective interest in certain goods. Such an interest can exist only with respect to "socially irreducible goods" (Taylor, 1995, p. 137ff.), that is, goods to which the group in question ascribes some profoundly communal, that is, non-individualizable meaning.[31] In that respect, not only that majority of the stipulated rights in the Draft Declaration are already protected by the existing international human rights instruments, but they can obviously be vested only in individuals. Such are, for instance, the right to life and the right to an adequate standard of living (Art. 3 of the Draft Declaration); the right to freedoms of association, opinion and expression (Art. 12), the right to have access to justice (Art. 13), as well as the right to information (Art. 7).[32] Some of the newly formulated rights, such as the right to seeds (Art. 5), the right to means of agricultural production (Art. 6); the freedom to determine prices and markets for agricultural production (Art. 8) are, again, directed primarily at addressing interest-based conflicts and protecting individual interests of members of a certain social category. Finally, there are some enlisted rights, such as the right to land and territory (Art. 4); the right to traditional agricultural knowledge and practice (Art. 5); the right to the protection of local agricultural values (Art. 9); the right to biological diversity (Art. 10); the right to preserve the environment (Art. 11), the right to food sovereignty (Art. 2.5),[33] as well as the right to participation in relevant decision-making processes (Art. 2.4)[34], which protect goods that might have the aforementioned communal meaning. The crucial question is whether there exists a stable community of peasants which shares such a meaning, worthy enough of generating a genuine and non-reducible collective interest in these goods.

30 For a more detailed elaboration, see Jovanović, pp. 110–119.

31 See *ibid.*, pp. 84–98.

32 Cf. Golay, pp. 10–12.

33 It is defined as "the right to healthy and culturally appropriate food produced through ecological sound and sustainable methods, and the right to define their own food and agriculture systems".

34 It is defined as "the right to participate in the policy design, decision making, implementation, and monitoring of any project, program or policy affecting their land and territories".

As already indicated, the very first problem that one is facing in the legal drafting of the personality of collective entities stems from a specific nature of putative right-holders, namely, that they are "*de facto*, pre-legally existing non-reducible collectivities." (Galenkamp. 1991, p. 297) In order to become legal right-bearers, these collectives have to be recognized as such by law. However, according to the aforementioned Heinze's scheme, the process of recognition implies that for the social construction of some relevant group identity, the step of group self-identification will not suffice. French sociologists, Poutignat and Streiff-Fenart, point in exactly the same direction in their inquiry of the social construction of ethnic identity. Namely, they say that ethnic identity is never defined in purely *endogene* terms, through the internally established conditions of "membership", but it is constructed in a dialectical relation to *exogene* definition, provided by non-group members. They call this dialectical process "categorial attributing" and this is what makes ethnicity a dynamic concept, subject to redefining and re-composition. (Poutignat, Streiff-Fenart, 1995, p. 155)

Claeys persuasively demonstrates that the ability of any social movement, including the one of peasants, "depends on 'meaning work': the production of meaning for constituents, antagonists and bystanders." (Claeys 2012, p. 847) In that respect,

> Rights talk (understood as "meaning work") plays a key role in the "reflexive process" of collective identity building. The active construction of a shared collective identity is crucial for mobilization because the unity of "people of the land" cannot be assumed. But identity is itself a goal of social movement activism. In an effort to gain acceptance for a stigmatized identity, Vía Campesina activists have called themselves "peasants" despite the pejorative connotation of the term. (Claeys 2012, p. 851)

It is clear that in some important respects "peasants" could be said to exist as a socially distinguishable category. However, it is doubtful, to say the least, whether this category shares all the social and cultural features of "groupness" attributed to them by the Draft Convention, such as the centrality of subsistence, the existence of a way of life based on household and community, the harmony with nature, the specificity of peasant behavior. For one, this definition fails "to depict the complex and evolving identity of contemporary rural families who often combine rural and urban, agricultural and non-agricultural, wage employment and self-employment", particularly in more developed parts of the world. (Claeys 2012, p. 854)[35] In less developed regions, where the struggle of the movement was instigated, the most

35 This is clear from interviews that Claeys conducted with representatives of farming communities from Europe. Notes, 16–18.

important claims were formulated primarily in social and economic terms.[36] Moreover, some of those claims that can be interpreted in identiterian terms, such as those to food sovereignty, land and territory, or specific cultural values, members of the peasant and rural communities can presumably already enjoy in the capacity of members of certain peoples, minorities or indigenous peoples. This, altogether, makes "peasants" for the moment incompletely qualified for the status of the right-holder of collective rights.

5. A Concluding Note

This essay aimed at clarifying some theoretical and practical problems regarding the conceptualization of collectives as a distinctive type of right-holders. While I argued that legal theory has enough material to perform this task, I also stressed that somewhat contradictory legal practice requires taking stance and grounding collective rights in the normative-moral view of value collectivism. At the same time, I demonstrated that, contrary to the view that nomotechnique is in the sole competence of political authorities, legal theory's work in tandem with social sciences is able to provide some useful general guidelines for the process of legal drafting of the personality of collective right-holders. Finally, using the case study of "peasants", I tried to show that the most pressing practical problem concerns the question which social entities possess the required features of "groupness" that make them apt for holding rights.

References

Bassen, Alexander, Jastram, Sarah, Meyer, Katrin (2005): ‚Corporate Social Responsibility – Eine Begriffserläuterung' *Zeitschrift für Wirtschafts- und Unternehmensethik* No. 6.

Bentham, Jeremy (1988): *The Principles of Morals and Legislation.* [1781]. Prometheus, Amherst.

36 This opens up the problem of strategic behavior of the movement. Claeyes has reservations towards the "peasants' rights" route of struggle. In her words, "the peasants' rights initiative may induce a shift in how La Via Campesina's struggle is framed in the future: not so much as an anti-capitalist struggle but as an anti-discrimination one. Will La Via Campesina put the emphasis on its transformative political project – and alternative societal project, food sovereignty – or on the distinctiveness of the peasantry? Making the struggle for peasants'rights too much about identity and recognition may damage La Via Campesina's long-term goals, if questions of redistribution are set aside." (Claeys 2013, p. 8)

Berry, Brian (2001): *Culture and Equality – An Egalitarian Critique of Multiculturalism.* Polity Press, Cambridge.

Bix, Brian (1993): *Law, Language, and Legal Determinacy.* Clarendon Press, Oxford.

Boshammer, Susanne (2003): *Gruppen, Rechte, Gerechtigkeit.* Walter de Gruyter, Berlin/New York.

Buchanan, Allen (1994): 'Liberalism and Group Rights' In: Coleman, Jules L., Buchanan, Allen Eds.: *Harm's Way – Essays in Honour of Joel Feinberg.* Cambridge University Press, Cambridge.

Bydlinski, Franz (1982): *Juristische Methodenlehre und Rechtsbegriff.* Springer, Wien/New York.

Claeys, Priscilla (2013): 'From Food Sovereignty to Peasants' Rights: An Overview of La Via Campesina's Rights-Based Claims over the Last 20 Years, International conference *Food Sovereignty: A Critical Dialogue*', Yale University, 14–15 September 2013, Conference Paper # 24: 1.

Claeys, Priscilla (2012): 'The Creation of New Rights by the Food Sovereignty Movement: The Challenge of Institutionalizing Subversion' *Sociology* 46.

Donaldson, Sue, Kymlicka, Will (2011): *Zoopolis – A Political Theory of Animal Rights*, Oxford University Press, Oxford.

Galenkamp, Marlies (1991): 'Collective Rights: Much Ado About Nothing?'. *Netherlands Quarterly for Human Rights* No. 9.

Golay, Christophe (2013): 'Legal Reflections on the Rights of Peasants and Other People Working in Rural Areas (Background paper)', Prepared for the first session of the working group on the rights of peasants and other people working in rural areas, 15–19 July 2013, available at http://www.ohchr.org/Documents/HRBodies/HRCouncil/WGPleasants/Golay.pdf.

Hartney, Michael (1991): 'Some Confusions Concerning Collective Rights' *Canadian Journal of Law and Jurisprudence* 4.

Heinze, Eric (1999): 'The Construction and Contingency of the Minority Concept' In: Fottrell, Deirdre, Bowring, Bill Eds.: *Minority and Group Rights in the New Millennium.* Martinus Nijhoff Publishers, The Hague.

Jones, Peter (1999) 'Group Rights and Group Oppression'. *Journal of Political Philosophy* No. 7.

Jovanović, Miodrag (2012): *Collective Rights – A Legal Theory.* Cambridge University Press, Cambridge.

Kymlicka, Will (1995). *Multicultural Citizenship – A Liberal Theory of Minority Rights.* Clarendon Press, Oxford.

May, Larry (2010): *Genocide – A Normative Account.* Cambridge University Press, Cambridge.

Mitnick, Eric J. (2006): *Rights, Groups, and Self-Invention (Group-Differentiated Rights in Liberal Theory).* Ashgate, Aldershot.

Narveson, Jan (1991): 'Collective Rights?' *Canadian Journal of Law and Jurisprudence* 4(2).

Noakes, Jeremy, Pridham, Geoffrey (1974): *Documents on Nazism 1919–1945.* Viking Press, New York.

Offe, Claus (1998): 'Homogeneity' and Constitutional Democracy: Coping with Identity Conflicts Through Group Rights' *Journal of Political Philosophy* No. 6.

Stone, Christopher D. (2010): *Should Trees Have Standing? Law, Morality, and the Environment* (3rd ed.). Oxford University Press, Oxford.

Sunstein, Cass R., Nussbaum, Martha C. Eds. (2004): *Animal Rights – Current Debates and New Directions*, Oxford University Press, Oxford.

Thornberry, Patrick (1991): *International Law and the Rights of Minorities.* Clarendon Press, Oxford.

Van Dyke, Vernon (1995): 'The Individual, the State, and Ethnic Communities in Political Theory' In: Kymlicka, Will Ed.: *The Rights of Minority Cultures.* Oxford University Press, Oxford.

Van Dyke, Vernon (1974): 'Human Rights and the Rights of Groups', *American Journal of Political Science* No. 18.

Tatiana Chauvin

Philosophical Anthropology as a Model of Human Legal Subjectivity

1. The right to legal subjectivity

Law as a system of norms plays an important role within every culture, most especially because of the extent and significance of its influence on the most fundamental aspects of every person's individual and social life. Its regulations guide human activity in minor civil and administrative matters as well as in political and public contexts. The very capacity for such agency is, in most cases, dependent on recognition of the individual as a subject by the binding law and his formal participation in the political organization governed by law. Awareness of the force of interaction and universality of legal norms, understood as a context of social functioning of individuals, is of fundamental significance in any attempt to sketch an image of man emerging from emerging from the law.

There is broad agreement among philosophers of law that the world depicted in legal texts is inadequate as a representation of the world as it depicts a virtually existing world. Nevertheless, one can surely reconstruct from legal regulations the legislator's level of knowledge and certain of their presuppositions about that reality (Broekman, 1993; Finnis, 1980; Radbruch, 2009; Jenkins, 1980). As Gustav Radbruch claims, on that same principle, law creates an abstract and general image of man that cannot capture is untranslatable into the understanding of humanity in its full richness (Radbruch, 2009, pp. 107–110). In the following text, I will attempt to significantly undermine this assumption, if not entirely rejecting it. Radbruch's assertion constitutes a confirmation of the specificity of ontological discourse that characterizes the humanistic approach to jurisprudence. By comparison with the natural sciences, the methodological status—or, indeed, existence—of the subject of humanistic discourse is weak. However, one might point out that the interest of the state in the individual, and consequently the legal regulations produced by the state, are not restricted to official data but attempt to grasp the essence (*eidos*) of humanity.

Positive law constitutes the "contours of the human world", outside of which a man is doomed (Nowak/Cern, 2008, p. 232). According to Hannah Arendt, the first step on the way to totalitarianism is extermination of the public person (legal subject) in the man (Arendt, 2012, p. 628). The uniqueness of legal subjectivity is that it may be comprehended as a kind of artifact, a prerequisite for maintaining real identity in circumstances under which that identity may be disturbed Broekman, 1993, p. 164). The protection of human dignity, individuality and autonomy may be efficient only when their possessor exists as *homo iuridicus* before the law.

According to Javier Hervada, the conceptualization of human subjectivity in law may be defined according to three non-mutually exclusive constructs: competency to possess rights and contract liabilities; owning a title to rights and obligations; and, finally, recognition of a subject as "being before the law" (Hervada, 2011, p. 106). The concept of a right plays a central role in contemporary normative systems. The right to be recognized as a legal subject is, in a way, the first in the order of rights of an individual; a precondition for their conceptualization and juridization. It constitutes a primary component of a mechanism that allows rights and obligations to be ascribed to the individual as subject of the law, simultaneously granting their possessor a remedy to exercise these rights (Bioy, 2013, p. 99). The right of recognition of legal subjectivity has been articulated, above all, in Article 6 of the Universal Declaration of Human Rights (*Everyone has the right to recognition everywhere as a person before the law*) and, on its basis, Article 16 of the International Covenant on Civil and Political Rights (*Everyone shall have the right to recognition everywhere as a person before the law*). However, this standard characterizes only these two documents; the Convention for the Protection of Human Rights and Fundamental Freedoms does not contain this norm and only obliges High Contracting Parties to ensure every man's jurisdiction rights and freedoms, as specified in Chapter I of The Convention (art. 1 ECHR).

Legal subjectivity is constructed as a right that inheres equally in all people. Its anthropological dimension is manifested in its strong relation to man (i.e., human person) as the subject of fundamental rights. A human being is a beneficiary of these rights by virtue of the value of the dignity that is correlated solely with his existence. It is this human dignity that entails ascription of the category of subject in social relations. As is frequently observed in reference to certain rights, relativization of the individual's position (by placing him in a concrete cultural, social, political, economic or religious context) remains within secure boundaries as long as it does not infringe this innate quality. The right to legal subjectivity, however, does not have the character of a natural right but originates in a specific obligation of the state to formally grant an individual the status of legal subject.

Summing up the conditions that constitute this status, Jan Broekman stated that modern western legal discourse is ruled by the vision of a man satisfying the following prerequisites (Broekman, 1993, p. 164): 1) law incorporates a man solely as a subject (individual, person); 2) that subjectivity is decided upon by qualities characterizing a man: the rationality, intentionality and transparency of his behavior (i.e., deeds and actions), based on supposition of free will, self-agency, responsibility and coherent biography; 3) subjectivity manifests itself in conflict situations and disturbed equilibrium—without this condition, the very existence of law could be undermined—and law plays a vital role in the necessary prevention or resolution of already existing conflicts; 4) law serves the subject by restoring violated equilibrium—it is no more than a transitional element, serving to restore balance—and for that reason, rights understood as remedies to vindicate claims are essential.

One can show the existence of the above discursive practices in every form of positive law. The necessity of recognizing a human being as an individual is evident in any particular legal settlement, as well as in the broader context/location as a legal subject in relation to others (public authorities, community and other individuals). The very basis of democratic society is the individual person, whose good constitutes the common good of the community to which he or she belongs (John Paul II, encyclical *Redemptor hominis* (17)). The restoration of balance is an objective of every legal decision; in contrast to political philosophy, whose leitmotif is war and evil, the fundamental motive of philosophy of law is the pursuit of peace (Ricoeur, 1995, p. 10).

The vital question of man concerns his existential condition and its global sense. The human mind-body structure is a constant source of various needs: material, psychological, emotional and cognitive. The most objective and universal of these are the minimal material needs related to existence, which must be satisfied for maintenance of the biological life and undisturbed development of every individual. In turn, within the scope conditioned by culture, an increasing subjectivism of needs and interrelated expectations is observed in relation to the state and its specific legal solutions (Mazurek, 2001, p. 283). In addition, there are secondary moral and ethical questions concerning the value of decisions made by a man, especially in the context of the ontological category of humankind.

Only an integrated conception of rights emanating from the integrally understood essence of human being might usefully address these complicated needs. Ascribing the status of person to a particular being entails recognition of their right to lay certain claims, such as right to life, corporal inviolability or autonomous development (Ricoeur, 2005, p. 452). This concept rests on the assumption that such characterized persons remain in a relationship based on a principle of mutual recognition, which is not merely a condition for the existence of a personal being but a response to the claim laid by this being as a person. Although that claim is admitted on the basis of certain characteristics of a species, recognition of somebody as a person is not dependent on the actual presence of these characteristics but solely on membership of the species (Spaemann, 2001, p. 6). Thus, the concept of a person does not serve the purpose of classification as a being but only affirms something that has already been defined (Spaemann, 2001, p. 9); as a basis for legal subjectivity, adoption of a specific anthropological model is required.

2. Relationship between law and anthropology

Four constantly recurring elements can be observed in the problematic relation between law and anthropology:

1) Reflection on the law and the state is a particular type of reflection on human being.
2) Practically every reflection focusing on the state and the law conceals its adequate representation of man, although this plays a crucial role.
3) In western civilization, especially since the Renaissance, positive law has followed from the transformation (i.e., reduction and semantic selection) of elements of a discourse on life. 4) The question of anthropology within law concerns the whole legal system and not just its selected disciplines (Broekman, 1993, p. 63).

Anthropological themes in law may be analyzed either as an underlying concept of man which is to be deduced by means of presuppositions, or as a concept of man emerging from fundamental legal regulations. In the first case, it is man that constitutes a fact warranting the whole legal order.[1] The sentence *Hominum causa omne ius constitutum sit,* from the Codex Hermogenianus (c. A.D. 293–294), remains the basis for the idea of law as a human measure [law immanent to people under its jurisdiction], coming into existence for his cause and because of him, as elaborated in the European legal tradition (Longchamps de Berier, 2012, pp. 129–130). On this approach, Man is a point of reference for the creation of various modal situations from which ensue absolute and relative rights. In the second case, man is an anthropological model constituted by law that an actually existent man is obliged to recognize and accept as one of his social roles.

---

1 See for instance Paul Amselek, followed by others in different variations (cf. Puppo, Alberto.: *Les fondements des systemes juridiques*, In: Koubi, Genevieve/Muller-Quoy, Isabelle (eds.), *Sur les fondements du droit public,* Bruxelle, 2003, p. 37). The term "foundation" means, in one interpretation, a "fact justifying" something, in another, it is a starting point in terms of logic (logical starting point).

Anthropological discourse, as a vision of global humankind, is partially implied in law as reasoning in accordance with rules of "application" typical of judicial discourse, as is the fundamental objective of legal reasoning and performance (Broekman, 1993, p. 29). Law is a specific way of thinking, speaking and acting, and even a specific form of existence. Legal regulations (normative utterances) may consider man a) as a person in their integrity (in which case law refers to a human, person, human person, everyone, no one); or b) in their distinguished social roles and functions (Böckenförde, 2006, p. 102).

The aspect of integrity of human person interest here is most often found in the provisions of constitutional law, standardizing fundamental rights (mainly personal rights, but also a substantial part of the rights of the second generation), and, to a significant extent, criminal law provisions. Anthropological assumptions are clearly starting point here. On the other hand, distinct social roles and functions are typical of administrative and civil legal regulations, where the assumption is that legal norms reconstruct the characteristics of human existence as individually and socially interpreted.

Nevertheless, as has already been pointed out above, the law does not fully capture our mode of existence. Legal discourse, like any moral discourse, usually aims to objectify and generalize the image of man, consequently falling short of the full scope of real human existence. In the area of morality this process enables subordination of human activity and experience to the area of normativity – that is, an area of stipulations above claims. Law, in serving not only an individual but also a political national community, "seizes" a man to grant him certain rights but also to place him beyond any individual order. What follows is a necessary reduction of individual needs and opportunities into universal marks of humankind that can be subjected to rationalization. The self-consciousness and uniqueness of each man that allows him to acknowledge himself as an agent, central to his experience of the world, has to surrender to the force of reductive operations that are based on a very strong teleological justification: that law, as a decision-making system of control and duress, has to construct an anthropological model that will assure its survival and consolidate its balance-recovering role.

Anthropology, as a law-founding discourse, remains implicit and yields to the artificial form of *homo iuridicus*. What confirms the strength of the bond that anthropology forms with modern western law is the fact that *homo iuridicus* is prerequisite for both the existence of the law and the boundaries of its sphere of influence. Law, with philosophy, is perhaps the only form of discourse legitimized by the image of man it constructs. In the end, it is difficult to point to a branch of the natural sciences or humanities for which reference to the essence of humanity would constitute a *sine qua non* of their existence (Broekman, 1993, p. 19) whereas in case of law, that reference is immediately evident.

3. The concept of man in light of selected standpoints in philosophical anthropology

The philosophical discursive tradition that, in my opinion, corresponds with the image of man emerging from legal regulations (mostly of public law, which I take to include constitutional, criminal and administrative law) is philosophical anthropology. The influence of anthropological assumptions in the decisions of legislators is very strong, although too rarely evoked *expressis verbis* (Jenkins, 1980, p. 314; Broekman, 1993, p. 81) What distinguishes the discussed type of anthropology from others (cultural and biological as well as pre-philosophical anthropology) is the content of questions and the manner of posing them, as well as the type of answers, in the context of fundamental philosophical problems (Paetzold, 1995, p. 465).

Taking under consideration all peculiar constituents of man, such as speech, body, self-agency, community, state, myth, religion and art, the main objective of philosophical anthropology is to determine man's position or standpoint in the world in relation to other beings (such as animals and God) and to nature, history and culture, in order to demonstrate what justifies this distinction from those others.

Two currents in philosophical anthropology are of particular interest here: the classical view, originating in German philosophy in the first decades of the twentieth century (represented by Max Scheler, Helmuth Plessner and Arnold Gehlen), and Christian personalism—especially the views of Jacques Maritain and Karol Wojtyła, who were both inspired, to a significant extent, by phenomenology and hermeneutics.[2] The quality that characterizes these two strands and binds them together is the so-called "eidetic attitude". Following Max Scheler, their precursor, the *de novo* idea of man they pursued was not a continuation of earlier philosophy but turned all previous traditions into an absolute *tabula rasa*, in which all normative aspects relating to studying the essence and aim of human existence were also to be discarded (Scheler, 1987).

These thinkers employed a peculiar methodology. They postulated recognition of scientific research as a source of knowledge about a man, equivalent to pure philosophical enunciations—one cannot separate man's experience from the

2 *Max Scheler*. In: Stanford Encyclopedia of Philosophy, from http://plato.stanford.edu/entries/scheler/#PhiAntMet.

essence of a man. On these grounds, their views are valuable in terms of legal discourse and criteria of legal subjectivity, as well as its fundamental characteristics formulated in accordance with the model "anthropology plus ethics" (or, in other words, descriptive plus normative anthropology) (König, 1983, pp. 269–270). Thus, from the point of view of functionality, one can speak of anthropological and personal functions of the law. The former concentrates on the protection of being (existence) and the inviolability of body and life; the latter consists in assuring an individual social status and appropriate subjective rights derived from the personality of a man, including both public and privacy rights.

First of all, then, philosophical anthropology centers on man, who is the supreme subject of its interest (Plessner, 2004, p. 26). Second, it reflects on its subject by reference to Dilthey's concepts of *Lebenswelt* and historicity, bringing argumentation other than purely the anthropological to bear on philosophical reflections on man (Paczkowska-Łagowska, 1994, p. VIII). Dilthey's heritage has enriched philosophical anthropology with its hermeneutical perspective, according to which a philosopher is first obliged to consider the issue of his community in the broad cultural context. The objective is a philosophy deeply rooted in culture, which is simultaneously its main premise (Lorenc, 2008, p. 15). By engaging with anthropological aspects, one reaches conclusions about the reality of surrounding world. The central place previously occupied by an abstract "being" is now taken by life as experienced. According to Gerd Haeffner, man always asks about himself today: the vision of a man as a subject is always correlated with a specific historic moment, even if it originates from and takes account of a wide philosophical heritage. Moreover, by virtue of his embodied nature, man experiences a temporality of being; an individual is a being "extended in time" between the origin and the end, situated in the natural world. Third, curricular respect for the biological perspective and the empirical sciences was to breach purely apriorical philosophical thought on what is typically human. These three characteristics confirm that these thinkers sought more than just a selection of features typical of solely apriorical or biological approaches.

The respective conceptions of these philosophers emphasize, to different extents, the personal status of man as relating to an essential aspect of his being and, with significant differences, his status as an agent.[3] A majority of them came to the recognition of man as person by comparison of his position in the world with

3 The concept of a man as a subject is most evident in the personalistic current, especially in writings of Karol Wojtyla. In the theories of the German anthropologists, it takes the form of particularly conceived self-knowledge (see: Scheler, Plessner).

the position of animals, which has encouraged some historians of philosophy to classify this current as naturalistic Hartman, 2006, p. 130). Indeed, animality is the fundamental categorical reference for definition of a man (Czerniak, 2002, p. 49). However, philosophical anthropology simultaneously renounces any connection with naturalistic reductionism, announcing man's excavation from Nature through the creation of a second nature, described by Plessner as "artificial": the world of symbols and values, where institutions, rights, beliefs or knowledge are possible (Hartman, 2006, p. 130).

Another important and widely explored topic is the problem of responsible life in the community and what might be called an anthropological category of socialization, where both strands of philosophical anthropology (classical and Christian personalist) approach a philosophy of dialogue. This is generally critical of currents promoting both individualism and collectivism, and proposes in their place a category of solidarism (*Scheler*), common good (*Maritain, Wojtyła*) or reciprocity rule (*Plessner, Höffe*).

One peculiar quality of the classical conceptions may, from a modern perspective, be perceived as a shortcoming. In reading the German thinkers, one might conclude that problems of dignity, liberty and free will, although present, were not of primary concern for some of them. It is difficult to explain the phenomenon as merely a desire to part with the tradition of one-sided conceptualizations of man that emphasize his autonomy or dignity as exhaustive categories of fundamental importance. Given the founding declarations of the newly established current, such a partition has never occurred. A possible explanation of the tenor of anthropological thought in the second and third decades of the last century is that the so-called "revolution of dignity" (Mazurek, 2001, p. 11) emerged as a consequence of the crimes of the Second World War. At the time of consolidation of the philosophical current in question, the issues of greatest importance were the challenges posed by scientific discoveries, so numerous in the nineteenth century, and consequent doubt about the human mind as an inviolable fortress (since Aristotle) of humanity. As has been pointed out in the literature, one reason for this latter concern was the demonstration of attributes of intelligence or sensitivity in other animal species.

It was not until the emergence of personalism in the second half of the twentieth century that these values became a fully integrative anthropological conception. This included the proclaimed ethical element, based on a particular idea of a person and his or her relationship with the perceived Stranger, according to the identical principle, as an equal in humanity. Personalism as a school of philosophical thought is based on the person as an entity of most particular status, superior to and transcending other entities. Personalistic reflection, as presented by Jacques Maritain and Karol Wojtyła, is evidently inspired by St. Thomas' concept of man as inclined to both good and evil. Invocation of the inclinations (Maritain) or of the essential role of experience in understanding the self and the outside world (Wojtyła) shows that morality should not be sought in externally conceived human nature (psychological, anthropological or theological), which is analyzed secondarily from the perspective of concepts based primarily in metaphysics.[4]

In the anthropology of Karol Wojtyła, and especially in the pre-pontifical writings, the personal nature of man is revealed in its correlation with freedom of behavior and its moral value. The human as agent (man-person) may deliberately choose good or evil, and that is of essential importance for the proposed concept of a subject of law, since an objective possibility of committing morally reprehensible actions is assumed (Wojtyła, 1979, p. 99[5]). Next, criminal evaluation of human behavior requires it to take the form of an act—an assumption of crucial significance for the theory and practice of criminal law. Nevertheless, man's capacity to perpetrate evil does not undermine his subjective (personal) status but, paradoxically, constitutes its confirmation, inscribing the capacity to do wrong into the legal anthropological construction. An objective is a person who has not recognized the truth (about good) as an internal rule of adjudication and decision-making (Wojtyła 1979, p. 181); at this point, moral judgment of the deed is of secondary importance.

It should not be left unsaid that, in compliance with this assumption, the issue of taking responsibility for one's actions also becomes an anthropological problem. Attribution of responsibility and, consequently, calling to account for it, is possible only when we deal with a subject primarily equipped with free will, capable of action by his essence and of taking responsibility in the original, ontic sense. Therefore, one should conclude that cultural and institutional context produce

4 The accuracy of this interpretation is proved by the reception of "Person and Act" by Karol Wojtyla. An important and recurring objection to his work was the adaptation in his anthropology of concepts of good, evil and human nature, well rooted in metaphysics. Cf. Wojtyła, Karol: Słowo końcowe po dyskusji nad "Osobą i czynem". In: Wojtyła, Karol: Osoba i czyn oraz inne studia antropologiczne, Lublin 2011.

5 "When we search deep into the integral structure of [...] man's becoming morally good or morally bad, we find in it the proper moment of freedom. It is in the structure of man's becoming, through his actions [...], that freedom manifests itself most appropriately. Here, however, freedom constitutes the root factor of the becoming as such of human morality."

only a kind of secondary conceptualization of responsibility resulting from man's very nature.

4. Anthropological subjectivity

The anthropological perspective on law shows that its norms and institutions form a system that has its source in particular anthropological apparatus and in the particular needs of man. Thus, at the basis of every political and legal conception there should be a concrete, though perhaps culturally neutral, denotation of man. This kind of "minimal anthropology" means accepting that the essence of man, in the broadest philosophical sense, is constructed from conditions that cannot be either "historicized" or "pluralized."[6] This view is frequently invoked as an argument for the possibility of defining universal human rights, as a consequence of a transcendent core of humankind that is shared by its all representatives.

Anthropological subjectivity, which on the account presented here constitutes a basis of legal subjectivity, assumes that human ways (areas) of existence are inseparably connected with fundamental dimensions or features of humankind. For Gerd Haeffner, they are essential in the sense that (Haeffner, 2006, p. 48): a) they fundamentally determine actual and possible ways of acting and modes of human existence; b) they affect people's understanding of themselves, either implicitly or through scientific cognitive research projects; c) they utilize possibilities of language; d) they occur not by monolog but in a social process, simultaneously emerging from and affecting social context; e) they correspond to particular opportunities, needs and restrictions of their time; and f) every science that centers on these "fundamental dimensions" has claimed a title of primary humanities (Haeffner offers the examples of structuralism, social and historical sciences).

According to Otfried Höffe, these fundamental characteristics include the fact that a man is a living being (biological, physical, striving for survival and health), equipped with abilities of speech and thinking and capable of cooperation and reciprocal coexistence (life in community). These three aspects jointly constitute man's capability to act (agency), together with its crucial feature: intentionality determining freedom. These are, Höffe continues, substantial interests, superior to the necessity of self-maintenance shared by all living organisms, and they are

6 Since the Enlightenment revolution of subjectivity, the essence of man can no longer be defined by its *telos* or desirable direction of self-realization in the manner of Aristotle, or by an a priori defined level of existence. See: Höffe, Otfried: *O antropologii praw człowieka*. In: Zajadło, Jerzy (eds.): Antologia tekstów dotyczących praw człowieka, Księga jubileuszowa Rzecznika Praw Obywatelskich, t. 3, Warszawa 2008, p. 670.

also constitutive of the moral self in man.[7] They are the only basis for universal claims and an equal share in dignity. In this sense, these are transcendent interests, the source of fundamental human rights. They cannot be dismissed on account of higher-order interests, nor can they be balanced, and their realization is only possible on the assumption of reciprocity. This canon must be complemented by a clear emphasis on the responsibility of the agent as a free individual, his recognition as a "center of action". Self-agency is to be understood as the ability to perform conscious actions in the surrounding world.

The connection of an anthropological image of man with his own vision of his own epoch is essentially a hermeneutic act,[8] and the only possible context for analysis of subjectivity. Thus, human consciousness of the temporality of being significantly affects the scope and form of human subjectivity, although a natural characteristic of all crucial decisions in this regard is their relative arbitrariness. Similarly, historicity constitutes another external perspective on subjectivity. As rightly observed by Gehlen, every theory of man should be considered in reference to its historical time (Gehlen, 2001, p. 93), simultaneously taking account of implications from the past. This time is determined, from one side, by the particular stage of knowledge in the natural sciences, and from the other by the condition of the humanities. Our understanding and explaining of subjectivity varies according to our current state of experience. At the same time, this process is dynamic; asking about man is always relativized to the current state of knowledge (specific and historical) and must be open to the possibility of change resulting from scientific progress and alternation of surroundings. The experience of historicity, to a certain extent, depends upon the axiological aspect of anthropological subjectivity. Man is contingent, temporarily being, posing temporarily relativized questions concerning both past and future. In respect of the latter, he is capable of deontological thinking, yet he cannot find the values he seeks in the material world to which he belongs. Human biological nature pertains only in very restricted degree to the realm of the good as ethically conceived. In order to establish actual conditions for the existence of values, man must create a new, "naturally artificial" cultural world that is more permanent than the biological life of a single man.

---

7 This inherent interest can be found beyond the conflict "physical or moral subject". The fact that one strives to survive while the other decides to sacrifice his life for political ideals will not be contradictory only if we assume that the one who makes such a sacrifice deliberately makes the decision about its circumstances. It is the only condition for maintenance of anthropological respect for life and health. Cf. O. Höffe.

8 It's enough to recall well known Dilthey's assertion: "What the man is, may be only told by his history."

5. Conclusion

The main objective of this paper is the attempt to confirm the intuition that the image of man as subject proposed by positive law has an eidetic dimension, linking it to philosophical anthropology. Each system of law originates from man and aims to represent his essence. This is evidence of the crucial correlation between man and his surroundings, which he must create for the sake of an inventive and safe existence. As a universal order, law aspires to complete the conception of man. Such a perspective imposes on legislators [law-creators] an adaptation of the anthropological model. In principle, the law exists to serve equally all its subordinates, without favoring a particular worldview or ideology. Certainly, this does not rule out necessary foundations in axiology, but the set of values realized by law is ultimately an outcome of the culture from which it emerges. Ideas of humanism and respect for human being, as proposed by Otfried Höffe's model (anthropology plus ethics), are found in the legal norms that regulate the position of man.

Humanity is difficult to define or even to place in a theoretical framework. Man cannot be a subject of definition in any sense; as an agent-interpreter and a definer, he is simultaneously the subject of his interest and an object of investigation. Nevertheless, even taking into account the thesis of the impossibility of exhaustive knowledge about man as propounded by many philosophers, one can seek to characterize his essence, accessible to intersubjective experience by reference to certain qualities uniquely typical of humankind. Based on these characteristics, legal systems of democratic countries and contemporary states ruled by law become a consequence of the recognition of inherent, innate human rights, the existence of which is fundamental to organized community and its institutional forms. For realization and full utilization of these rights, they must be formally reflected in the regulations of positive law. At the same time, membership of a particular legal culture obliges legislators to respect value systems established by the international community, offering as an object of protection a concept of man that would include his fundamental characteristics, including both the basic needs of existence and the natural urge for development. Man conceptualizes his own image in law according to his time. Today, he is perceived above all as a being predestined to individual fulfillment and protection. Simultaneously, the fact of membership of a community obliges legislators to include in the legal regulations provisions that favor the harmony of social life.

None of the characteristics discussed above can be considered as prior to any other since, as Helmuth Plessner warns, all attempts to reduce human nature to one decisive factor—whether spiritual, rational or biological—are doomed to failure. This cannot be achieved even by man himself through self-experience, as any such attempt will be no more than a mere echo of all that might be said about a man. Nevertheless, the rule of arbitrary law requires us to acknowledge that some aspects of man must be relatively permanent in character. The main concern is to ensure that the norms that organize and regulate human existence to function as a relatively inviolable system of references and values that permit shared legitimization. The essence of man, in all its openness and unpredictability, must be translated into a language, a social task involving the consolidation of a specified, culturally determined vision. Consequently, finding relatively sustainable and reliable characteristics is necessary for maintenance and protection of this vision.

Perhaps, then, it may be concluded that the law has found an answer to the question that has long troubled philosophers, namely "Who is the man?" Although that seems doubtful, the law's unquestionable merit is its attempt to construct a universal anthropological project, in which man as a vulnerable being would find shelter and scope as a rational and naturally free person, which are the conditions for fulfillment. At a time when philosophy has questioned the existence of a subject, it is the law that has a constant obligation to restore man to his proper position, emphasizing, maintaining and enhancing subjectivity. This belief is shared by Norbert Rouland, who proclaims law's contribution to the "resurrection" of a subject (Rouland, 1991, p. 24). For that reason, the meaning of the question of the nature of being a man, and of how his humanity may be protected and developed under moral imperatives and legal norms, should be constantly revisited.

The schematism of the language of legal acts disguises anthropology, whose aim must be to meet the requirements of the many forms of human being (polymorphism), manifesting itself simultaneously in the spiritual and biological dimensions and corresponding to the function of law in the social and individual order. In the face of more and increasingly significant interference with the physical integrity of human beings, and the consequent difficulties in maintaining the biological boundaries of humanity, we are obliged to seek a philosophical basis of legal subjectivity that will meet the objective of respecting this vision.

References

Arendt, Hannah (2012): *Korzenie totalitaryzmu*, Warszawa.

Bioy, Xavier (2013): 'Le droit a la personnalité juridique' In: Bioy, Xavier Ed. *La personnalité juridique*, Toulouse.

Böckenförde, Ernst-Wolfgang (2006): 'Wizerunek człowieka w świetle dzisiejszego porządku prawnego' In: Michalski, Krzysztof Ed. *Człowiek w nauce współczesnej. Rozmowy w Castel Gandolfo*, Kraków.

Broekman, Jan M. (1993): *Droit et anthropologie*. Paris-Bruxelles.

Czerniak, Stanisław (2002): *Lorenz, Plessner, Habermas. Dylematy antropologiczne filozofii współczesnej*, Toruń.

Finnis, John (1980): *Natural Law and Natural Rights*, Oxford University Press.

Gehlen, Arnold (2001): *W kręgu antropologii i psychologii społecznej. Studia*, Warszawa.

Haeffner, Gerd (2006): *Wprowadzenie do antropologii filozoficznej*, Kraków.

Hartman, Jan (2006): *Wstęp do filozofii*, Warszawa.

Hervada, Javier (2011): *Prawo naturalne. Wprowadzenie*. Kraków.

Höffe, Otfried (2008): 'O antropologii praw człowieka' In*:* Zajadło, Jerzy Ed.: *Antologia tekstów dotyczących praw człowieka, Księga jubileuszowa Rzecznika Praw Obywatelskich*, t. 3, Warszawa.

Jenkins, Iredell (1980): *Social Order and the Limits of Law*. Princeton N.J., Princeton University Press.

John Paul II, encyclica *Redemptor hominis* (17).

König, Eckard (1983): 'Czy koniec antropologii filozoficznej?' *Studia filozoficzne* 213–214 (8–9).

Longchamps de Berier, Franciszek (2012): 'Podmiot prawa: między Rzymem a Jerozolimą' In: *Konsul est iris et patriae defensor. Księga pamiątkowa dedykowana doktorowi Andrzejowi Kremerowi*, Warszawa.

Lorenc, Włodzimierz (2008): *Hermeneutyczne koncepcje człowieka 2, Dilthey, Misch, Bollnow*, Warszawa.

Mazurek, Franciszek, M. (2001): *Godność osoby ludzkiej podstawą praw człowieka*, Wrocław.

Ricoeur, Paul (2005): *O sobie samym jako o innym*. Warszawa.

Nowak, Ewa, Cern, Karolina M. (2008): *Ethos w życiu publicznym*, Warszawa.

Paetzold, Heinz (1995): 'Człowiek' In: Martens, Ekkehard, Schnädelbach, Herbert Eds.: *Filozofia. Podstawowe pytania*, Warszawa.

Plessner, Helmuth (2004): 'Zadanie antropologii filozoficznej' In: Czerniak, Stanisław, Rolewski, Jarosław Eds.: *Antropologia filozoficzna. Studia z filozofii niemieckiej*, Vol. 4, Toruń.

Paczkowska-Łagowska, Elżbieta (1994): 'Wstęp. Natura ludzka, historia, polityka w antropologii Helmutha Plessnera' In: Plessner, Helmuth: *Władza a natura ludzka. Esej o antropologii światopoglądu historycznego*. Warszawa.

Puppo, Alberto (2003): 'Les fondements des systemes juridiques' In: Koubi, Genevieve, Muller-Quoy, Isabelle Eds. *Sur les fondements du droit public*, Bruxelles.

Radbruch, Gustav (2009): *Filozofia prawa*, Warszawa.

Ricoeur, Paul (1995): *Le Juste 1*. Paris.

Rouland, Norbert (1991): *Aux confin de droit. Anthropologie juridique de la modernité*, Paris.

Scheler, Max (1987): *Pisma z antropologii filozoficznej i teorii wiedzy*, Warszawa.

Spaemann, Robert (2001): *Osoby. O różnicy między czymś a kimś*. Warszawa.

Wojtyła, Karol, (1979): 'The Acting Person' In: *Analecta Husserliana*, vol. 10, The Reidel Publishing Company, Dordrecht, Boston.

Wojtyła, Karol (2011): *Osoba i czyn oraz inne studia antropologiczne*, Lublin.

Antonio Cota Marçal and Paula Maria Nasser Cury

The Constitutive Journey Toward Individual Personhood

1. The human being as a rational agent

Among the various self-conceptions elaborated by the so-called occidental man, the one with Aristotelian origins has surely been the most persistent. Even if not always explicitly labeled *Aristotelian*, many of its features are still widespread in the contemporaneity.

As with any philosophical thesis, the Aristotelian has been subject to various sorts of criticism and interpretation. What we claim here is only that, in its core elements, it is still influential in the present days, guiding and being used as a reference for other conceptions elaborated by the man about himself, even in law. However, if, on the one hand, these elements reflect a pragmatic dimension that is present in the conception of personhood we take to be the most appropriate; on the other hand, we do not subscribe to certain forms of recourse to Aristotle that can still be found in contemporary literature, committed to his metaphysics or with an instrumental use of his thought for different purposes.

Either way, it seems to be beyond dispute that the Aristotelian conception about the human and its subsequent Latin uptake have forged the vocabulary related to the issue, whose meanings were constituted and delimitated in the perspective of the sociopolitical and cultural realities, respectively, of ancient Greece and Rome. The same holds true for the integrative process of assimilation and appropriation of that conception from the Hebraic-Christian theological and anthropological standpoints. Although not very usual in the Neoplatonic phase of the Patristic, the notion played a central role in the subsequent instrumentalization of the Aristotelian thought by the Christian theology of Boethius, and even more with Thomas Aquinas. Even the several attempts at disrupting the prevailing theology in the Middle Ages have not been able to provide a fundamentally different explanation of the human.

It was only in the sociopolitical and cultural modernity that alternative conceptions began to compete with the Aristotelian and its versions, including the religious ones. By sociopolitical and cultural modernity, we mean a set of different events, such as the end of the papal suzerainty upon the institutions of civil society and the new ambit of the exercise of rationality in the individual sphere, the emergency and politicization of a personal autonomous and free individuality, and the constitution of experimental science as the intersubjective and self-corrective exercise of a reason that can be shared by all human rational agents.

Although Aristotle takes it that the human being has various sensuous and physiological functions in common with other animals, he constantly emphasizes the existence of elements distinguishing and specifying the human as such. In particular, only humans could have *logos*, understood as reason, language, argumentation or reasoning, and capacity to express and justify, in the presence of others, a relational content they identify and conceptualize, an underwritten statement, an action performed, knowledge, and experience. The human being would accordingly be the only animal capable of theorizing, of giving reasons and justifications that count as grounded rational knowledge, and of knowing herself, other humans, and the world by means of reasons which are discursively justifiable and objectifiable in the processual dynamics of rationality and of reality itself. A so-constituted sapience is intersubjectively shareable and refutable by reasons and justifications that can be either extracted from the observation of things and facts or derived from the human agent acting upon herself, the other human beings, or the surrounding environment. Furthermore, the human animal would be able to express, in a linguistically articulated and universalizable fashion, relations among data and facts, or even among mental states, making them also intersubjectively objective and, as a consequence, shareable, criticizable, and reformulatable by other human beings. Because this knowledge or *episteme*, as the product of an intersubjective elaboration, is rationally constructed, facts and knowledge regarding new relations and arguments can deconstruct that previous knowledge, modify it, and, accordingly, make it advance or regress. It is a facet of the realistic dimension of Aristotelianism, as opposed to Platonism as well as to the later idealization of the Aristotelian thought.

In his Perì Psūchês, translated to Latin as *De Anima*[1], Aristotle affirms that thinking and knowing, *logos* and *nous*, identify the human being as such. After considering that substance can be either matter or the form able to turn matter into a determined being, or a being as composed of matter and form, Aristotle assumes that matter is potency, while form is the actualization or the fulfillment

---

1 *De Anima* was used as the Latin translation of *psique* possibly because there was no other Latin word corresponding exactly to the Greek one, or maybe because of the correlation between the Latin verb *animare* (to provide with air, to make live, to provide something with meaning or character) and movement as a principle of the action, or even under influence of the Hebraic "blow" (*nephesh*, *ruach*, and *neshamah*) (Georges 2010a, pp. 434–435).

of a potentiality. In this sense, Aristotle considers the interrelation between matter and form as producing both knowledge itself and the exercise of that resultant capacity (Aristotle 1952, p. 642)—in other words, the intellect, or the ability to know, and its exercise. After regarding all natural living bodies as composed substances, Aristotle assumes that "the soul cannot be without a body, while it cannot be a body; it is not a body but something relative to a body" (*Ibid*, p. 644). Furthermore, Aristotle says that "If thinking is like perceiving, it must be either a process in which the soul is acted upon by what is capable of being thought, or a process different from but analogous to that", and adds: "Thus that in the soul which is called mind (by mind I mean that whereby the soul thinks and judges) is, before it thinks, not actually any real thing. For this reason it cannot reasonably be regarded as blended with the body." Aristotle concludes that "once the mind has become each set of its possible objects [...], its condition is still one of potentiality, but in a different sense from the potentiality which preceded the acquisition of knowledge by learning or discovery: the mind too is then able to think itself" (*Ibid*, p. 661).

Despite that realistic dimension, it cannot be ignored that the Platonic idealism reappears in some features of the Aristotelian thought, leading to contradictions. For example, for what reason does Aristotle affirm, in the above-mentioned work, that the *psique* is immaterial? How can immateriality be compatible with being in a material body and making use of it to act and exist as an agent? Could not rationality be considered as another function of the psique itself—maybe its most complex function?

Yet it can be noticed that, unlike Plato, Aristotle does not isolate the soul and its function from the physical and material conditions and states of humans and animals. Indeed, he considers psychology as a part of physics. Once more, however, it is questionable that Aristotle offers a defense of metaphysics, named *first philosophy* or *theology*, as the apex of a theoretical knowledge whose object is simply an eternal and absolute form as the first and last grounding of all that is real or possible, a pure, static act which is distinguished from all the others, in a word: god. In summary, would that mean that Platonism is inevitable as the only form of rationally possible knowledge? Or would other kinds of knowledge, supposedly extrahuman and not objectifiable from the rational-scientific standpoint, be presupposed as necessary for a better explanation of the human?

Despite those contradictions, Aristotle is able to provide a concept of the man as a rational human agent who can identify relations among data, facts, and events, as well as among individuals and institutions, and also relations among relations. It also means being able to act with and upon the other humans and the environment in which she finds herself, including being able to think and act due to purposes and goals defined by that agent for herself and in relation to the others. It also means, therefore, following norms or standards and being liable to answer for the consequences of one's own actions.

2. Rational agency as constitutive of human personhood

Well before Aristotle formulated his conception about the human being as a rational agent, another characterization, compatible with the Aristotelian, had already been developed in the Greek cultural universe and expanded to the Romans. In the sphere of theater and also in the space of the rational constitution of society and language, certain features of the social practices were made explicit, such as roles and functions, among other rational intersubjective performances. Those elements, particularly in theatrical practices and later in the wider field of life in society, led to the deployment of the term *prosopon* to characterize the appropriately stylized and robed human individual as exercising the function of actor in a theatrical representation.

According to Benseler (1896, p. 736), the Greek term *prosopon*, generally used in plural even if referring to an individual person, means "face, physiognomy, visage, or countenance." It also meant mask or a represented role, when referring to theatrical players, their costumes, and accessories especially chosen by one to play the role of a certain character—therefore, a third person in contrast with the actor and the spectator. In another meaning, *prosopon* designated an interposed person that would act defending the interests of another, something like a legitimate representative or appointee. The Roman version of *prosopon* was *persona*, whose etymological origin is still disputable. However, the Latin language itself provides elements to understand the term as designating the same phenomenon as the Greek *prosopon*, in the same field of activity or in analogous ones. *Persona*, according to the explanation, would be a word formed by the preposition *per* (through, over or along something) plus the verb *sonare* (sound, resonate, rumble, vibrate). Thus, behind the mask or persona, the actor's performance and actions would let and make the represented character manifest herself, her actions, and their results. It can be therefore noticed that it is in and through action, specifically rational action, that the agent constitutes herself and can be identified as a person.

When, in the second century before Christ, the first grammar of the Greek language was created in Alexandria by Dionysius Thrax (Gudeman 1909, pp. 21–61, pp. 96–98), the grammatical concept of person incorporated the senses of first, second, and third pronominal and verbal persons that were already experienced in human discursive practices. From the theatrical, literary, and sociopolitical roles played by the authors and actors resulted socially and linguistically made explicit that the person was that agent who is the author of her own actions and performances and, by acting or playing a role, undertakes roles and functions in the society within which she becomes herself. In this regard, Thiel, for example, emphasizes that "'*Persona*' was then used to denote this role or character itself, and its denotation was transferred from the role on the stage to the role or function that an individual human being fulfills in real life" (Thiel 2011, p. 26).

When the concept started being used in Greek and, later on, in Roman social practices, respectively, *prosopon* and *persona* incorporated and expressed, implicitly, what would afterwards be named the capacity to be a holder of rights and duties. And that capacity would derive precisely from the fact, even if inexplicit, that the subject in question was a rational agent who is able to distinguish between right and wrong, to evaluate and choose ends and means, as well as to predict and evaluate the consequences of her theoretical and practical actions. Subsequent registers point to an occasional deployment of *persona* as a reference also to collectivities or corporations, in a way considered the precursor of the current concept of juridical person (Fuhrmann 2010, p. 25450). Of course, we do not presuppose here a self-consciousness on the part of authors and actors as in the later Cartesian and Lockean versions.

In accordance with that prevailing understanding, being human and being a person were, therefore, different concepts, related to one another to the extent that the *persona* would designate certain roles or characteristics of the human agent, of her functions and actions, conferring to her a social recognition (Kirste 2015)—which, as a matter of fact, cannot be considered complete. Even if a *persona* were held responsible for her performance, even legally responsible, that could not mean a broad recognition of her autonomy and freedom, since the notion of individuality was still incipient, and the personal identity had not yet been constituted and integrated to the social practices.

Three concepts based on the exercise of relevant functions and roles were constituted after these first moments of the journey toward individual personhood. Those concepts are related to actions and functions performed by rational agents in interaction, namely: actor, author, and authority, in Latin, *actor*, *auctor*, and *auctoritas*, respectively (Georges, 2010a, pp. 92–93, 703–708). *Actor*, the actor, derives from *agere*, which means "to act, to play a role." In playing a role, the agent-actor primarily represents the character of another agent and, in her way, makes the action of that other agent be present and comprehensible to the spectator. Certainly, her ability and creativity, as well as her knowledge and interpretation of the character, can interfere with the final product, modifying it or making it be faithful to what is being represented in a larger or smaller scale. In this sense, one is and can surely be an actor in all and every human activity, not only in theater.

Auctor, the author, is in turn derived from *auctus*, the past participle of *augere*, which means "to add, to make grow, to promote, to aggregate." By acting as an author, the agent creates something, not necessarily only an idea or a text. She innovates, prospers, adds something or some value to what was already available to her. Similarly, one is and can be an author in various activities performed in the interactions with others.

Finally, *auctoritas*, authority, also derives from *augere*. The agent invested with authority is not only that which adds and makes something prosper in which she is an authority, but also the agent from whom one can expect innovation and aggregation of value or improvement in her area of activity. She is, however and above all, the agent who has competence, knowledge, or experience, which she can use not only to dictate or write commands, but also especially to rationally awaken and motivate intelligences, minds, and capacities. An authority must have and aggregate the elements constitutive of actors and authors to the ones she possesses for being an authority: she must play roles, be an author, besides having competence in what comes to the knowledge and experience necessary to make other rational agents act. Thus, neither was authority conceived as synonymous for power, nor the terms that designate them coincide. Power is expressed in Latin by the word *potestas*, which means "the capacity of force and effectivity upon someone or to do something." In Rome, the only ones who had such power were the agents of the highest administrative hierarchy, such as rulers or distinguished members of public administration.

3. Person as a simile of god or god as a simile of the human agent as a person?

The dimension of an intersubjectively exercised and procedurally constituted rationality, present in the previously mentioned conceptions of *logos*, ended up being set aside in the subsequent period. Factors that led to this were, on the one side, the incorporation of the Neoplatonic-Plotinian line of thought by the ascending Christianity, which gave it a suprarational, idealistic, and eminently dogmatic connotation. On the other side, this way of understanding the religious phenomenon was reinforced by the dissemination of a morality with a Manichaean mind-set, promoting the disqualification of the mundane and the corporeal by dichotomically opposing both the concepts of good and evil and the concepts of spirituality and matter. These two factors were not isolated from one another. Rather, they reinforced themselves mutually as the Platonic idea that the body is the prison of the soul was undertaken, accentuating the disqualification of human corporeity. The situational world, as well as physiological sensations and perceptions, came to be directly related to the evil and the sin. As seems evident, this comparatively more restricted view about the *logos* influenced the way in which the concept of person was received and given a new meaning by this incipient tradition.

In the process of propagation and explanation of its beliefs, Christianity had to deal with two fundamental questions or antinomies of its doctrine: the paradox of a single god which is triune (father, son, and holy ghost as different persons of one god that is singular in its genus, species, nature, or essence); and the duality of natures between the divine character *son* and the human character Jesus, both coexisting in one only and very same person. The first thinkers or theologians did not find terminological references considered sufficient or complete about the persons of trinity in the Bible, especially in the Old Testament. The concepts and respective relational contents of *prosopon/persona*, which had been previously imported from grammatical studies as exegetic tools in the comprehension of the roles performed by the narrator of a text, by her interlocutors and by those to whom the interlocution refers, were consequently transported to the heart of the Christian dogmatic itself. As trinitarian persons, father and son were, thus, conceived through the relations and performances of the first and second persons. Tertullian (160–220 a.C.) is usually identified as the first one to think of the holy ghost as an interlocutor between father and son (Fuhrmann, p. 25458). This way, it was assumed that recourse to the relations comprehended by the functions and roles constitutive of *prosopon*, *upostasis*, and *ousia* and their Latin correlates *persona*, *substantia*, and *natura* would make it possible to theologically elucidate the dogmas expressed by the formulas "three persons—one substance" and "two natures—one person or individual" (Fuhrmann, p. 25458). Simultaneously, it was sought to avoid incurring in the Plotinian hierarchical unevenness between the One, the Intellect or *Nous*, and the Soul of the World.

The problem to be solved was to conjugate the individuality that distinguishes persons from one another with the coparticipation of different persons in one and the same divine nature, as well as with the possibility of coexistence of a divine and a human nature in just one person. Relations identified on the basis of roles or functions of the *persona* were an initial reference, which, however, became gradually forgotten due to the deployment of philosophical and/or exclusively religious concepts by theologists. Nonetheless, the ignored relations were the ones actually shaping human interaction. The imposed solution was that which considered rationality as the connecting element between the divine and the human, that is, as the form according to which the divine could participate in the human, and the human in divine reason, considered superior. To Boethius belongs the theological concept of person that, based on philosophical concepts, predominantly Aristotelian, such as nature, rationality, and substance, seemed to better meet the pursued goals: *persona est naturae rationalibils individua substantia* (Boethius 1998, p. 75).

Whether such a resumption of rationality and individuality is a sufficient explanation for the existence of one and the same person in the presence of two rational natures—one divine and the other, human—is a problem that the well-accepted Boethian solution left unanswered. On the other side, since what is at stake are entities (the one and triune god) considered absolute and unchangeable, the question about the possibility that finite and contingent relations, such as functions and roles in the human social praxis, be able to make explicit and comprehensible the religious or mystic absolute, without extrapolating the intersubjectively exercised rationality, also lacks a satisfactory answer. Moreover, would not the result of all those efforts be merely the creation of an absolute in the image and likeness of the human?

It is also recurrently said that, in the Scholastic (from the 11th to the 17th century), a special *dignity*, proper and distinctive of the human, was brought to light. This is another issue in which ambiguity, partiality, selectivity, exclusion, incoherence, and contradiction are involved. Indeed, the concept of dignity was dealt with in a blurred way, not only regarding linguistic practices, but also in an operative and pragmatic sense, most of the times managing to make the social and individual games obey the ecclesiastical commands. The fact is that even Giambatista Vicco and Giovanni Pico Della Mirandolla shared the belief about the creation of the human in the image and likeness of god.

Already in Rome, *dignitas* was predominantly associated with individual political performance, to the respect and recognition in virtue of the merit resultant from actions for the benefit of the community. It could also result from the visibility of belonging to nobility or exercising a public function, from the pomp and appearance, from a distinguished lifestyle. It was a simultaneously political and moral concept, also associated, for this reason, to humanity and magnanimity. Pöschl emphasizes that in Rome, vindication of a distinguished status and commitment to the benefit of the community were always associated in such a way that the *dignitas* conferred on one by the community's recognition depended on the subject's performances. In this regard, Pöschl mentions the figure of the censor as a representative of the community to monitor the dignity of the senators. It can be noticed that, for the Romans, *dignitas* was not only a privilege or a private law, but also a moral norm to be followed (Pöschl 2004, pp. 637–645).

Another important feature of the further development of the conception of dignity in the Middle Ages is the fact that, for the Romans, it would be impossible to conceive a sociopolitical order without level and category distinctions, expressed either in titles and functions or in social classes and the establishment of a hierarchy. Since the religious and political consolidation of Christianity was also carried out upon the Roman basis, many of the Roman administrative institutions and even the terms that designated them were transposed to the Christian universe. Although it was primarily a religious institution, Christianity, thus, turned out to show similarities with imperial Rome: an absolute monarchy, titles, and functions that were proper of the Romans, different hierarchical levels, a strictly centralized authority, and a discipline oriented to the moral-religious control of body and mind. Some scholastics argued that such control had the function of restoring what had been lost by sin, since the dignity conferred on men due to their similitude with god would lie in their possession of reason and in their freedom of the will. As an institution that was also human, Christianity was not able to keep itself away from vanity, pomp, and magnificence, that is, from the identification of dignity with wealth, honorary titles, prestige, and ostentation. In this concern, it cannot even be considered an example of respect for autonomy and individual freedom in the exercise of the religious power or authority it attributed to itself.

In medieval Christian theology, even in the golden times of Scholastic, dignity is therefore grounded, ultimately, in the doctrinaire belief about human creation in the image and likeness of god, being, in addition, subjected to ecclesiastic management.

In the analysis of the Christian construction of the concept of person, it is worth noting that the theological recourse to terms like *nature*, *rationality*, and *substance* at the same time reflects the deployment of Aristotelian concepts like *physis*, *logos*, and *ousia*, but eliminates from them important features of his thought. It can be thus seen as an instrumental use, in order to ensure the maintenance of a purely religious belief in a divine person based on the more palpable idea of human person, instead of consistently justifying the belief. Such a construction culminates, in our understanding, in an anthropomorphization of the very entity held as divine, in its individualization accomplished by an approximation with the human character. The instrumentalism becomes even more evident if we observe that, in the name of the belief and despite its theology, the actions and practices of institutional Christianity ended up denying the very human person, her individual freedom, and the proclaimed resultant dignity.

After all, the political-religious practices adopted by Christianity along centuries, placing itself in a position to dictate the good and the evil, ended up overwhelming the manifestation of human individuality, in a way that makes it worth questioning: in practice, what individual substance was that to whom the character of person was attributed? Only the divine? Has the constructed person ended up denying both its constructor and the human reality taken as reference or model? Where is the rationality of the substance taken as reference and, consequently, its autonomy and responsibility to be found? How can the punishment of someone who is not treated as autonomous and responsible in her action be rationally justified? This sort of behavior led to clear actions of denial of freedom, to exclusion and annulment of the other precisely in the ambit of the exercise of reason, which concerns the stipulation of what is good or evil and, as a result, what the subject believes in and how she conducts her life. Instruments of denial, in this sense, go from excommunication (*ex* = expel, exclude) to the death penalty, sometimes in the most sadist ways, as in the bonfires of inquisition. Because of all that, arguments that the contemporary conception of person as a being endowed with a special dignity, or that the actual human rights derived from this dignity have their roots in the biblical texts as well as in the theological conception of *persona*, including the development of the figure of the *persona moralis*, can only be regarded as merely formal.

What Christianity really added to the previously existent concept of person is, therefore, restricted to the explanation of the alleged existence of the theological figures of trinity on the basis of the category of individual substance, at the same time that the divinity is identified with an infinite potentiation of human attributes and proprieties. Besides that, what such concept brings to light is an attempt to substitute Neoplatonic categories for a reading inspired by Aristotle of the Christian dogmas and beliefs, which, nevertheless, eliminates from Aristotelianism its pragmatic dimension.

4. The emergence of the person as a personal individuality in human society

From the 11th century onward, a series of events contributed to the slow but continuous resumption of the autonomous and intersubjective exercise of rationality, rehabilitating and amplifying the dimensions of *logos* and also of *ethos* in the individual and public spheres. Consequently, another step was taken toward the self-conception of the person as a rational agent.

The first among these events were the crusades. Motivated by religious impulses or political ambitions, they ended up confronting the Christian Europeans with peoples, religions, and cultures different from theirs. The first different, in this sense, was the Orthodox Byzantine and, in the sequence, the Islamist Arabian, both considered infidel for following religions held as not true, although equally derived from Judaism. The experience of the different, especially of the other as another human agent, gave the Europeans a deeper self-knowledge, as well as the chance to better know and to relativize the beliefs and culture proper of their own lifestyle.

The coexistence with those others, although most times in the form of contraposition and struggle, showed the Europeans that other ways of living were possible, even when based upon different beliefs and conceptions about god, the truth, the good, the evil, the correct, and a whole range of values. It also became possible for them to be aware of the limits of their knowledge and to get informed about new technologies and knowledge in areas not very developed in Europe, such as mathematics, medicine, and astronomy, and even philosophy and its relations to theology. Other Aristotelian texts and a different reading of them by Arabian philosophers came to the attention of the Europeans and contributed to a renovation of Christian theology on a different basis than Platonism. In the legal ambit, the collaboration and confrontation with the remaining Byzantine Empire allowed the assimilation and dissemination of Justinian law, usually known as Roman law, which began to gradually compete with and take the place of canonic law. The same happened in relation to an institution that the Europeans came to know and to develop under the name of university, which was already present in Constantinople as in what are today is Morocco and Egypt (Goody 2008, pp. 253–265; see also Marçal and Cury 2012). This first and long-lasting event reinforced the constitutive processes of self-identity and personal individuality.

Another important event was the progressive consolidation of differences and similarities among the multiple confessional entities that belonged to the Holy Roman Empire (962–1806). Effects of that distinctive consolidation were the disintegration of the Caesaropapism, which had its height in the time between the papacies of Innocent III (1198–1216) and Boniface VIII (1294–1303); the captivity of the seven subsequent popes in Avignon under the custody of the French kings; and, lastly, the Great Schism period (1378–1417) in which there were simultaneously two popes (1378), and three since 1409 (Geiss 2002, pp. 382–384, p. 403, p. 409). In its convocation, objective, and decisions, the Council of Constance (1414–1418) portrayed the contradictions and the transition in course: assembled by one of the three popes under the pressure of the Hungarian king Sigismund, the council convicted Jan Hus as a heretic and, as such, he was burned alive. It also convicted the already dead in 1384 John Wycliffe to have his bones burned; deposed Pope John XXIII; and led Pope Gregory XII to renounce and Spain to withdraw support for the third pope, Benedict XIII, culminating in his renunciation. The events express the effectuation of national individuality and self-identity and are reflected in the gradual formation of a great part of the current European national states and of their cultural identity in areas like language, art, legislation, and the respective social practices, and even the religious ones.

The third event, which, in part, was a cause of the previous one and happened simultaneously, consisted of the different movements toward a reformation of the papacy and the return to the initial beliefs and practices of Christianity, taken to have been distorted along the previous centuries. The Cathars, known since 1143 and had spread through France, England, and the north of Italy, as well as the Waldensian (1176), were persecuted by the inquisition and exterminated in a crusade initiated by Innocent III. Many were the reformers, among which were Gioacchino da Fiore (1135–1202), John Wycliffe (1330–1384) in England, Jan Hus (1370–1415) in Czechoslovakia, Girolamo Savanarola (1452–1498), Ulrich Zwingli (1484–1531), Thomas Münzer (1490–1525), Jean Cauvin (1509–1564), and Giordano Bruno (1548–1600). Martin Luther (1483–1546) was the most successful one, partly because of new political and religious conditions at his time. The attempt at allowing the believer to think of her own religion supported by reasons that she herself identifies is a characteristic common to all movements and reformers, although almost all of them ended up relying upon something similar to dogmas. Nonetheless, they all shared an opposition to the dogmatic and authoritarian imposition of beliefs by a select group, and to their practices, considered contradictory to what they claimed their beliefs were. In Lutheranism, there is an explicit appeal to the individual, who is responsible for her salvation or conviction. It is at this point that the individual, each and every one, begins to have the possibility of assuming the role of protagonist in the religious ambit.

Simultaneously to all previous events and similarly to what was happening with Roman Christianity, some people, already critical or discordant of the masks used by the sociopolitical organization to which they belonged, began to think for themselves and to look for alternatives, turning particularly to the intersubjectively grounded rational knowledge. Since everything was explained and interpreted as the product of god's initiative—at times kind and communicative via revelation, at others wrathful and brutal via plague, climatic changes, and other punishments for an alleged sin— the dissidents found another way to deal with the problems and questions raised by their own experiences: to confront what they had learned and that was established with what they observed and experimented, to discuss the reasons given, and to look for better explanations and justifications, especially those based on better rational and intersubjective grounds. Criticism, disagreement, progresses, and throwbacks; reasons and counter-reasons; experiences; daring to innovate, contest, and dialogue; reviewing one's own positions and reasons; an openness to the different and unknown; the creation of new hypotheses—all of these done successively until an adequate solution could be found. It was the constitution of modern experimental science as a dynamic and permanent construction, which is self-corrective and elaborates laws and theories instead of doctrines and dogmas. This way, a new reference pattern for rationality was designed in which individuality and personal identity could be literally and factually politicized, that is, started integrating themselves to the social practices and guiding them.

Cultural and political phenomena, products of the newly opened perspectives, were the humanism of the Renaissance, the rediscovery of the classical antiquity and of the periods before it, the re-readings of Plato and Aristotle, the unveiling of myths such as the one attributed to Lorenzo Valla in regard of the testament of Constantine in benefit of Christianity, the Enlightenment, and the improvement of philosophical discussions about politics and what would become the modern State. Thinking and the manifestations of thoughts came, thus, to meet a new space of autonomy and freedom, although threats still existed.

Another side of the same process, which, despite the conflicts, resulted in significant effectuations of autonomy and freedom of the national states and of the individual human agents, was the long and fratricide European wars, above all the religious ones. The first major European war, the Hundred Years War (1337–1453), involved France, England, and their respective allies. Its legacy is considered to be the crisis of feudalism due to the loss of prestige of the knights, nobles who fought for their king or suzerain. Four religious wars, in particular, deserve to be mentioned: the wars of Kappel (1529–1531), the Schmalkaldic War (1546–1547), the war against the Huguenots (1562–1598), and the Thirty Years' War (1618–1648). The results and advances of these and other events were gradually effectuated, beginning with the Treaty of Westphalia (1648), underwritten respectively with France in Münster and with Sweden in Osnabrück. Some of its highlights were the extension of the Peace of Augsburg (1555) to the Calvinists, the confessional parity in the legislative commissions and judicial chambers, and the prohibition of majoritarian decisions in disputes of confessional character. Not less important were the recognition of the independence of Switzerland and Netherlands and the ratification of the treaty and its implementation despite its reprobation by Pope Innocent X, which was ignored. Indeed, the Treaty of Westphalia declared not only the autonomy and independence of the national states, but also their autonomy from any religious authority. Secularization had begun, the European religious unity was over, and the presence of a relative linguistic, political, and cultural multiplicity could already be noticed. The way to a greater acknowledgement of personal individuality and of the rights of the individual person, as well as to the progressive constitution of the democratic state of law, was opened with the Enlightenment by the end of the 18th century and the so-called bourgeois revolutions: the English concluded in 1689, the American in 1776, and the French in 1789. Rights became recognized and posited, and clearer limits for individuals and states were defined. Science and philosophy, religion and theology became autonomous in relation to one another and the first ones started being guided by a rational objectivity, which was intersubjectively constituted and aware of both its limitations and the procedural character of its development and self-correction.[2]

5. Individual personhood as a self-construction from the social-normative institutive practices

The elucidation of the elements around which, since the Modern, individual personhood is being constituted provided the tools for the formulation of a contemporary approach to conceptual objectivity as a phenomenon instituted in a rational and intersubjectively articulated process.

One of the findings that support such an approach to objectivity is that exercising the role of actor or author in various practices performed by rational beings is something that can be made explicit in terms of a normative pragmatism. The action that counts as rationally intelligible, distinguished from other responsive human or nonhuman attitudes in face of stimuli, is the one that inserts the agent in the normative-evaluative dimension in which his responsive performance implies the mastery and application of conceptual contents, thus enabling the agent to autonomously take a stand on multiple issues. In that dimension, being an individual self is, itself, a status socially instituted as the agent is assessed and recognized as "a subject of perception and action, one who can both be committed and can take others to be committed" (Brandom 1998, p. 559). The possibility of

---

2 A fundamental role in this process was played by Locke, Hume, and Hegel. Locke was the first one who drew attention to the problem of the persistence of individuality along the time, emphasizing the functions of self-consciousness and memory. With Hume, a significant turn to the empirical condition of knowledge, of conscience, and even of the agency opens the way to a more critical conception of the human. In Hegel, the concept of agency is a central feature in his system, since it is through action that the individual becomes self-conscious of herself and of the other individuals, who, in turn, also acquire self-consciousness in this interaction. It is in this interactive process that social practices, institutions, the state, beliefs, knowledge, values, rights, and duties are produced, in a permanent individual and social constitutive process.

practically individuating selves according to those normative features assumes a central structural role in rationality, since selves "correspond to coresponsibility classes or bundles of deontic states and attitudes" and, as such, are the ones who can enter the spaces of reasons (Brandom 1998, p. 559).

In this sense, both the action performed by uttering a speech act and the action performed by taking up a certain practical attitude involve evaluations of correction by the agent and the attribution and undertaking of commitments and entitlements that support the practiced action and insert it in a justificatory network of public reasons. Such reasons, on their turn, also consist in evaluations of correction, as well as in attributions or assumptions of commitments and entitlements on the part of the other agents. According to such perspective, what distinguishes rational action from other practices is the conceptual articulation of the former, giving it the aptitude to serve as reasons that consist in a criterion of correction for subsequent inferences and, at the same time, when challenged, demands reasons sufficient to justify it as correct. It is important to notice that this capacity of mapping the reasons which justify the theoretical use or the practical application of conceptual contents is, simultaneously, what confers meaning on them. And, by conferring meaning, a self leaves the mark of her individual personhood in the experienced reality.

Undertaking that thesis implies endorsing the consequent notion of a semantic holism, insofar as it is only in terms of further concepts, presupposed by or derived from the application of a given concept, that the content of this original concept can be determined. Normative pragmatism and semantic holism show a necessary interconnection if we notice that the meaning of that given concept is instituted by the various agents-persons through social practices governed by attributions and undertakings of entitlements to its use and of commitments to the presuppositions and consequences involved in its application. Rationality is exercised insofar as, conjugating those dimensions, we are able to explain what we are doing in applying a concept and to evaluate as correct or incorrect the application in judgments, in the exercise of a choice, and even when responsively reacting to natural and social events (*Ibid*, p. 592).

It follows that the criteria of correction and the possibility of sharing a conceptual content, although we can start from different premises and extract from it distinct conclusions, are instituted in the intersubjective action, in the social practices of taking or treating something as correct or appropriate. From the confrontation between those subjective normative attitudes, which makes personal individuality even more explicit by evincing the existence of different perspectives about what is taken or treated as correct relatively to the same concept, it becomes possible to distinguish between conceptual applications evaluated by a certain subject as correct (because he takes it that the necessary entitlements are present and, thus, that the commitments undertaken by the concept user herself would be justified) and what is, from our point of view, objectively correct in regard of the concept, that is, the effective commitments and entitlements which, from our perspective, should have been inferred from it. Since this dynamics of normative attitudes and evaluations of correction is intersubjective or, in other words, multilateral, what we judge as objectively correct from our point of view also consists, from the point of view of other interlocutors, in a subjective normative attitude whose objective validity, in turn, will be evaluated in light of the criteria of correction inferred by those interlocutors.

From that dynamics results that the difference between subjective normative attitudes and what is objectively taken as correct becomes a question of social confrontation between perspectives, which emerges in the exercise of intersubjectivity. In Brandom's words: "On this account, objectivity is a structural aspect of the social-perspectival *form* of conceptual contents. The permanent possibility of a distinction between how things *are* and how they are *taken* to be by some interlocutor is built into the social-inferential articulation of concepts" (*Ibid*, p. 597). Accordingly, objectivity is understood in terms of the form the process of social articulation of concepts assumes, not of the conceptual contents themselves. A conceptual content is seen not as a preexistent datum which is necessary for the application of the concepts, but as a construction originated in the social practices of concept use, which, through the confrontation of perspectives, is constantly open to actualizations and reviews. In this sense, what integrates the conceptual contents, also of concepts like human being, person, and individual, is permanently constituted through its public applications.

Opposite to contents aprioristically attributed to concepts by theological dogma or other sorts of authoritatively imposed beliefs or norms, what is at stake is an essentially democratic and intersubjective constitutive process, which gives back to the individuals the role of protagonists in the spaces of social coexistence, recognizing them in their freedom and autonomy. Self and person, according to this point of view, are thus predicates that the agent constructs insofar as she goes on exercising those functions. The same holds, for example, for the concepts of individuality or individual. According to a minimal definition, an individual is necessarily the one who is self-conscious as identical with oneself and distinguished from the others and, as such, can be distinguished from everyone and everything else. In a first moment, the necessary character of that definition can denote certain staticity. The threat of staticity dissolves, however, once the minimal semantic core, a necessary part of the content conveyed by the concept of individual, is also immersed in the above-mentioned procedural-pragmatic dimension, insofar as that distinction by negation is seen as an always ongoing, dynamic, and mutable process, in which the individual comes to be, at each moment, what she, due to her own intersubjective action, makes of herself. Indeed, no conceptual content is given to our knowledge with an aprioristic meaning; meanings are just *what we give them* by using them in a way or another in our social practices.

6. Conclusion: from individual personhood to depersonalization?

In the different areas of our study—namely, scientific knowledge, coherent action from the ethical standpoint, and participation in the public space as a rational agent—the currently available practices and technologies allow for a better capacitation of the exercised social roles, both as an individual person and as a community of individuals. Nonetheless, the knowledge and the corresponding techniques are still concentrated in the hands of few and lack a greater effectuation, since the states, up to whom it primarily is to provide access to the basic instruments for the development of life in social interaction, do not undertake that function as their own. As a consequence, an opposite way of personalization ends up being followed: the individual becomes frequently treated as part of a mass, and not in her individuality and singularity. The submission of continents and peoples throughout the world to colonialism and imperialism replicated the medieval denial of the other and of the culturally different ones. The traces and consequences of those policies can still be noticed in political, economical, and social relations among single states and internationally. A generalized developmental deficit in the conceptions of state, authority, and citizenship, and a lack of openness to the new and to the other as a different individual, is associated with a predominantly authoritarian and subservient mind-set that traces back to premodern religious and institutional frameworks. Various factors contribute to the deficit, from the inability of different educational systems in what comes to the qualification of the subjects as agents critical of their own reality to the insistence of a kind of legal formalism that is unsustainable as a rational discursive practice.

In the predominantly capitalist contemporary society, the individual, who is theoretically recognized as a citizen, a holder of the state of law, a constructor of the state and of law, and their ultimate end, is nonetheless increasingly treated as an object in practice. This objectification happens in either her relation to the state of law itself—many times masked by the appearance of legitimacy an alleged democratic legislation confers on its acts—or her relation to the other citizens, at work, in the condition of taxpayer, of a user of what the state is obliged to provide, and, more generally, in the spaces of conduction of her individual life. Another reflex of that is the loss of control upon privacy due to actions and omissions by the state itself, which at the same time violates these limits and refrains from elaborating norms that would actually preclude the perpetuation of such practice. An individual under those conditions is easily catchable by ideologies of various sorts, weakening, for this very reason, her self-identity and her capacity of self-determination. Moreover, with globalization and the increasing complexity of the relations among the states and the individuals in different aspects such as the economic, the political, and the cultural, the unprepared individual does not feel safe or does not control her future anymore—a consequence of the loss of control upon her own present. It all ends up generating a tendency to the marginalization of individuals in relation to the available interactional processes.

The unpreparedness perpetuates the contradiction between the self-promulgated Christian moral of the West and the practices of denial of the person that are still carried out locally and even globally. Thus rationally, intersubjectively, and pragmatically speaking, it is no wonder that those local and global actors continue creating fictions and masks, including juridical ones, to avoid others from noticing their self-contradiction and not to let their authentic and real *personae* emerge. How could privileges in the legal international order otherwise be explained, as illustrated by the current composition of the security council of the United Nations and its right to raise a veto? Or the selective application of compulsory norms and sanctions? Are we really experiencing an authentically democratic and global representation? What is ultimately at stake: the correct and the good, or the private interests of certain states and colligations? What should we say, for example, about the wars in Afghanistan and Iraq, of the current scenario in Syria, of the frequent episodes of xenophobia and racism by physical and juridical persons, of the explicitly interests-oriented implementation of the international disarmament policy, of the renewed dispute between the NATO and Russia for hegemony in their respective areas of influence?

It urges that the law, as a social practice that claims scientificity, does not incorporate the discourse in denial of the person, many times translated into authoritatively imposed legal norms in the national and international scenarios. In this sense, the law would have to be effectively (and not just ideally) constituted with the involvement of its addressees, as direct or indirect authors of the norms in a democratic state of law. On the other side, it is important that the law assumes its rationality and scientificity, ceasing to rely on patterns and values, in sum, on concepts that have already been overcome, turning itself more incisively to the reality with which it deals. A condition for it is that the law releases itself from its linguistic and epistemic self-imprisonment and, instead, opens itself to the multiversity, which should be the object of its area of activity. Nonetheless, it cannot be expected only from institutions that they recognize that way of acting and have the initiative to implement it. It also depends on the individual that she affirms herself as a person, claiming for the application of that knowledge and for accountability about things and processes for which society itself pays.

In view of the presented arguments, the answer to the leading question of this essay – in what does individual personhood ultimately consist? – seems, thus, to be that it is an ongoing process. Assuming the processuality constitutive of the person raises, however, new questions, for which other answers still need to be constructed. After all, do we have control over that process, or have we instead lost or even never had such control? Are we moving toward not being autonomous, free, and responsible persons? Or will we, at some point, find ourselves in a new stage, which is currently unknown to us? Has the human always been like that without noticing it? Or, is it really the individual who is constructing herself and defining the stages she has gone through and the ones she will still go through? To what extent is this self-construction, elaborated on the basis of elements held to be exclusively human, not a claim which excludes other possible forms of personhood?

Engaging in such a discussion and trying to answer those questions, giving reasons, confronting arguments and practices considered to be inappropriate, ultimately undertaking the commitments, vindicating the entitlements necessary to support a certain position, and demanding that the interlocutors also act that way are, simultaneously, to assume one's own individual personhood and to promote its semantic-pragmatic actualization.

References

Aristotle (1952): 'De Anima' In: *Great Books of Western World*, Vol. 8, Encyclopaedia Britannica Inc. William Benton Publisher: Chicago-London-Toronto.

Benseler, Gustav E. (1896): *Griechisch-Deutsches Schul-Wörterbuch*. 10. Auflage. Druck und Verlag von B. G. Teubner: Leipzig.

Boethius (1998): 'Contra Euthycen'. In: Elsässer Michael Ed.: *Die Theologischen Traktate: lateinisch-deutsch*. Meiner: Hamburg.

Brandom, Robert (1998): *Making it Explicit: reasoning, representing, and discursive commitment*. Harvard University Press: Cambridge.

Fuhrmann, Manfred (2010): 'Person' In: Ritter Joachim, Gründer Karlfried, Gabriel Gottfried Eds. *Historisches Wörterbuch der Philosophie*: Volltext CD-ROM des Gesamtwerkes. Schwabe: Basel.

Geiss, Immanuel (2002): *Geschichte Griffbereit*, Bd. 4. Wissen Media Verlag: Gütersloh/München.

Georges, Karl E. (2010a): *Ausführliches Lateinisch-Deutsches Wörterbuch*, 8. Auflage. Darmstadt: Wissenschaftliche Buchgesellschaft.

Goody, J. (2008): *O roubo da história*. Contexto: São Paulo.

Gudeman, Alfred (1909): *Grundriss der Geschichte der klassisschen Philologie*, 2. Auflage. Druck und Verlag von B. G. Teubner: Leipzig und Berlin.

Kirste, Stephan (2015): 'Die beiden Seiten der Maske – Rechtstheorie und Rechtsethik der Rechtsperson'. In: Kirste Stephan, Gröschner Rolf, Lembcke Oliver Eds.: *Person und Rechtsperson. Zur Ideengeschichte der Personalität*. Mohr: Tübingen.

Marçal, Antonio Cota, Cury Paula Maria Nasser (2012): 'Ethics and science in the Brazilian legal discourse', 25th IVR World Congress: Science, Law, and Technology. Paper Series n. 086/2012, Series D, Frankfurt a.M. 2012, from http://publikationen.ub.uni-frankfurt.de/frontdoor/index/index/docId/24944.

Pöschl, Viktor (2004): 'Würde im antiken Rom'. In: Brunner Otto, Conze Werner, Kosellek Reinhardt Eds. *Geschichtliche Grundbegriffe. Historisches Lexikon zur politisch-sozialen Sprache in Deutschland*. Studienausgabe, Vol. 7. Klett-Cotta: Stuttgart.

Thiel, Udo (2011): *The early modern subject: self-consciousness and personal identity from Descartes to Hume*. Oxford University Press: Oxford [u.a.].

Tomasz Pietrzykowski

Beyond Personhood: From Two Conceptions of Rights to Two Kinds of Right-Holders*

1. Two Theories of Rights

The long debate over the concept of rights is widely known. The so-called Interest Theory of Rights has been advanced by, i.a., Jeremy Bentham, Rudolf von Jehring, Joseph Raz, Neil MacCormick, and recently, Matthew H. Kramer. The proponents of the competing Will Theory include such names as Bernard Windscheid, Herbert L. A. Hart, Nigel Simmonds, or Hillel Steiner. Both theories continue to attract supporters and remain in use until today.

According to the Interest Theory, the essence of a right is the legal protection of the right-holder's interest. Legal rights correspond to some duties of others constraining freedom to infringe on the interest protected by a given right. Thus, having a right means to be the beneficiary of a duty imposed for the sake of the good (interest) of the right-holder. The main weakness of this account of rights is difficulty in distinguishing genuine rights from cases in which someone's benefit is a mere reflection (a side-effect) of somebody else's duty. Second, someone may possess a legal right despite having no actual interest in holding it (neither preferring nor having any clear benefit from the protection she is provided with).

The alternative theory of rights, the so-called Will Theory (or Choice-Theory), claims that having a right means being entitled to choose freely from some available options. An essential point of having a right is not protection of interests, but rather exercise one's freedom of will. A right-holder is conferred with some range of control over duties of others (authorized to trigger or waive such duties). A legal right is not a mere passive protection but rather a delegation of active powers to make discretionary use of some duty-imposing rules.

The basic problems with the Will Theory arise in respect to the situations of incompetent right-holders (such as infants, mentally ill etc.). It is difficult to claim that the law authorizes such persons to exercise their will to control the duties of others. It would mean, therefore, that such persons could not have any legal rights. It is also difficult to reconcile the Will Theory with some of the so-called

* This paper has been prepared for the research project financed by the Polish National Center of Science (2012/07/B/HS5/03957).

inalienable rights, held and legally enforced irrespective of the will of their fully competent beneficiaries.

There are numerous arguments invented for and against both of these traditional theories of rights. There are also many interesting proposals to define rights in terms of various combinations of interest and will. However, I am not going to examine them here. Instead, I will try to approach this debate from another perspective. Namely, I am going to argue that the ambiguity of the meaning of legal rights may shed some important light on our understanding of the nature of personhood in law (usually identified with the capability to hold legal rights).

2. Rules, Normative Situations, and Positive Legal Rights

There may be legitimate doubts concerning the very nature of the traditional controversy between the "theories" of rights. Is it a clash of two views on the objective nature of some entities called "rights"? Or is it an argument about the proper use of words according to prevailing linguistic conventions? Or rather the combat of stipulative definitions based on pragmatic or moral reasons? What kind of legal consequences depend on whether one refers to some normative situation as a "legal right"? These questions reflect a much wider problem of the nature and place of conceptual analysis among the methods to elucidate reality, in particular, legal reality (Pietrzykowski 2011).

In my opinion, any plausible approach to the discussion of the nature of legal rights has to rely on some basic naturalist assumptions. At least in respect to legal rights resulting from rules imposed by the lawmaker (as it takes place in modern civil law systems), there is hardly any sense in arguing about the nature of rights as something beyond the shape of normative situations created by relevant rules of law and reflected in attitudes and patterns of behavior of norm-addresses. Thus, a positive legal right is a combination of behavioral and mental attitudes of norm-users shaped largely by the content of rules constituting a normative situation of a certain type (Pietrzykowski 2015a).

From this point of view, arguably there are just two different types of normative situations that are ordinarily referred to as "rights". Each of them underlies one of the main theories of rights that take one type of such situation as *the* model of what rights *actually are*. But it is doubtful whether there are any reasons to hold that there is just one normative situation that exclusively deserved to be referred to as the genuine "right". There seems to be rather two parallel conceptions of legal rights corresponding to two different types of normative situations that legal rules commonly create. Neither of these conceptions are wrong in any other sense than not meeting criteria of being a true "right" set forth by the opposing theory of what rights actually are.

3. Differing Normative Situations

It is obvious that legal rules create various normative situations and serve different purposes. Clearly, in some cases rules of law are enacted to protect the interest of some subjects of law. In order to do so, they impose constraints (duties) to secure respect for some subjective interests that the lawmaker finds deserving of legal protection. This protection may often be constructed to apply relatively independently of the will or preferences of those whose interests they are meant to serve.

Many such situations are explicitly labeled "rights" directly by the lawmaker. In many other cases this qualification may be imposed by the norm-users (legal doctrine and judicial interpretation of the rules in question). It is not difficult to find any number of practical examples of this kind of rights. According to the Polish Constitution: "The Republic of Poland shall ensure the legal protection of the life of every human being" (art. 38). This legal rule aims to protect what the lawmaker finds as a basic and vital interest of every human being – namely, life. It is a provision placed in the chapter entitled *Personal Freedoms and Rights* and is commonly (including the Constitutional Court) described as the "right to life").

There are many similar examples of constitutional and statutory rights established to protect what the lawmaker takes to be an objective interest of the beneficiary rather than one's freedom to control the corresponding duties of others. An interesting case may be an employee's rights to remuneration or to safe conditions at work. Both of these rights cannot be effectively waived by the choice of the employee who is supposed to be their beneficiary. Any infringement of the employer's duty is considered to be a breach of the rights of the "harmed" employee and the latter is not able to make any effective declarations to waive protection.

No direct legal consequences seem to depend on their being called a "right" rather than a "protection" of some objective value or interests of the subjects intended as beneficiaries of such protection. Even if incidentally it may have some interpretive relevance, as a matter of principle the meaning and effects of the relevant rules hardly depend on whether or not they are conceptually qualified as a "right". In a normative situation of this type, the existence and scope of legal constraints is largely independent of the subjective preferences of each particular beneficiary. The decisions regarding which interests should be protected and how to effectuate it are authoritatively made by the lawmaker. Undoubtedly, in real world such decisions shall never perfectly fit to the actual interests and expectations of all those intended to be protected by the legally imposed constraints.

On the other hand, there are numerous situations in which legal rules confer an entity (right-holder) with powers to bring about some legal effects (and in this way exercise some scope of discretionary control over duties of others). Thus, the right-holder becomes authorized to freely choose how to use this power in order to pursue goals and interests in the subjectively preferred manner. Typical examples may be the right to vote, to execute or terminate a legally binding agreement, to bring an action to the court, or to marry another person.

In this type of situation, the lawmaker does not determine in advance the way in which the interests of a given class of right-holders should be protected. It rather makes the manner of such protection dependent on the their own choices and preferences. This principal difference is, to some extent, obscured by the fact that, in the first type of situation, the authoritative constraints against harmful behavior may often concern only actions that are contrary to the will of the right-holders (the intended beneficiaries of the legal protection). For example, the right to bodily integrity or freedom from sexual harassment only prohibits acts that are unwanted by the right-holders. In practice, the violation of the right also depends ultimately on the will of the right-holder. Nonetheless, the preferences of the right-holder do not influence the existence of a legal right (exerting effects beyond the control of the right-holder), but partially define the act constituting its infringement.[1]

Both types of normative situations are created in practically all branches of law. Constitutional rights may belong to one or the other type. Penal code may provide protection that is effective irrespectively of the will or choices of the beneficiary, as well as protection operating in a manner close to the model of freedom to trigger or waive available legal protection. Both kinds of situations may also be found in private law (e.g. family matters) where at least some interests may be protected despite the will of those on whom the protection is conferred.

4. Against *the* Concept of Rights

The existence of the above types of normative situations underlies the ambiguity of the concept of rights that is deeply embedded in the legal discourse. It is not clear why the only one of such situations should be regarded as representing a genuine right (and what it could actually mean in this context). One may equally accept that there are just two conceptions of rights the co-existence of which reflects two different types of normative situations by virtue of which law is used to serve its addresses.

1 In other words, the right-holder is not authorized to claim that despite rights being infringed upon, the legal effects shall not follow (the right shall not be exercised).

Arguably, there seems to be a substantial difference between moral or natural rights and legal right in this respect. In the moral (philosophical) discourse, rights are typically believed to exist irrespective of any rules established, or even explicitly declared, by any authority. Hence, the accepted conceptual conditions of the existence of a right are essential for the identification of what rights exist and what follows from their existence. In modern systems of positive law the legal rights, however, derive principally from the rules specifying who is entitled or obliged to do what. It means that contrary to moral (natural) rights, in case of rights constructed by rules of positive law the normative status of a conduct is determined mainly by the content of applicable rules and not by an independent conceptual qualification of the situation in the agent.

For example, the provisions of the Polish Constitution say that each citizen of Poland while staying abroad has "the right" to be protected by the Polish state. The existence of such rights (as the Constitution dubs it), as well as legal consequences it entails, are determined mainly by the content of detailed applicable regulations and only secondary to the conceptual qualification of such protection as a right. Another example may be constitutional rule providing that "the inviolability of the home shall be ensured". The duties, claims, and other legal effects of this provision (as specified in detail by other rules of various codes and statutes) are, as a matter of principle, the same whether or not one tends to consider this rule as establishing a legal right.

Even if the distinction between both types of normative situations representing two conceptions of rights admits of degrees, most practical cases of legal rights clearly fall within the scope of one or the other type. Following the traditional vocabulary I will call them "Interest Rights" and "Choice Rights", respectively.

5. From Types of Rights to Kinds of Right-holders

An important implication of the distinction between Interest Rights and Choice Rights is the difference between the conditions of their ascription. Interest Rights may be plausibly conferred to holders who are capable of having their own subjective interests. If some of such interests are found deserving legal protection the lawmaker may decide to effectuate it by imposing constraints on the behavior of others (or the interest-holder herself). To benefit from having Interest Rights, the holder does not have to be aware of being conferred with them, let alone be able to deliberately invoke or enforce the effects they give rise to.

In respect to these kinds of rights, the key question is then: what are interests and who can be regarded as an entity capable of having them? I believe that it is not a matter of conceptual inquiry, but rather a deep substantive problem of normative ethics. It actually concerns one of the most fundamental questions of moral philosophy, that is, who should morally count and why.

For obvious reasons, I am not able to examine such a paramount ethical problem within the scope of this paper. I will limit myself to briefly outlining the approach to which I subscribe. It is deeply skeptical about any explanations founded on speculative contemplation based on beliefs in any kind of metaphysical realm of abstract objective values (somehow levitating above the empirical world in a kind of platonic supra-reality). Instead of that it prefers explanation of the moral aspect of reality in terms of naturally evolved predispositions of some creatures to experience state of affairs as attractive or aversive.

`Those living organisms that have developed sufficiently complex nervous systems, are able to sense their environment and strive to care for themselves by intentionally pursuing and avoiding what they perceive as desirable or harmful. Due to such capacity, their life acquires a new subjectively evaluative dimension. The affective valence related to the subjective well-being is an ultimate underpinning of further cultural conventions of human morality transforming it in various ways into the realm of moral norms, values, and attitudes. All good is ultimately and necessarily a good for someone (a sentient creature). The concept of the good is inherently "tethered" (as Ch. Korsgaard puts it) to a creature able to experience the reality as subjectively better or worse (Korsgaard 2013).

Together with the ability to experience reality as subjectively better or worse, sentient creatures begin to have subjective interests in having their lives as good as possible (Korsgaard 2012). A necessary and sufficient condition to have one's own interest is having a rudimentary first-person perspective enabling one to perceive states of affairs as subjectively valent (Baker 2013). The scope and variety of such affectively positive and negative sensations become multiplied by the development of self-awareness and culture. Due to this fact human perceptions and experiences of value are considerably more sophisticated than even their closest kin. Nonetheless, these basic interests are held even by relatively simple non-human animals capable of subjectively experiencing the world. Their interests reflect the positive and negative desires determined by their needs and goals they naturally strive for.

The conditions of the reasonable conferral of Choice Rights are significantly different. This conception of right entails powers the holder has to be able to exercise. Thus, holding it implies not only capability of having subjective interests but also competence to make decisions how to make use of the conferred right to pursue those interests. It does not rule out, however, that incidentally such rights may be held also by individuals actually incompetent (temporarily or permanently) to practically exercise them if only the relevant decisions could be made on their behalf by competent third persons. Nonetheless, it would seem inconsistent with the nature of Choice Rights to ascribe them to the creatures that are in principle unable to make use of the relevant powers.

While normative situations corresponding to Choice Rights are typically more complex than those behind Interests Rights, the latter often relate to the most basic, essential needs of the right-holders. Part of the reason why in some cases the lawmaker decides to establish Interests Rights rather than Choice Rights seems to be the belief that there are so basic and universal interests that they can be hardly disregarded by any of the potential right-holders. Some level of protection of their elementary interests is indispensable to benefit from having any additional Choice Rights. Those Interest Rights that provide right-holders with some basic protection of their vital interests I will call "elementary rights".[2] Taking into account that exercising Choice Rights involves mental qualities traditionally associated with the concept of person, I will refer to this type of rights as "personal rights".

Using this terminology, one may conclude that elementary rights may (and should) be ascribed to all creatures able to have subjective interests that may deserve legal protection. To this extent, there is no reason to make the position of a right-holder in any way dependent on the capacity to possess and exercise any additional personal rights. Therefore, it seems that at least two main kinds of right-holders should be distinguished. The first includes creatures apt to have only some of their interests protected by means of elementary rights (if only the lawmaker finds sufficient moral reasons to grant them such protection). The second consists of creatures capable of holding both elementary and personal rights.

To address this difference, full persons in law should be distinguished not only from things but also from non-personal subjects of law (pertaining to creatures able to have just some elementary rights). Insofar as non-personal subjects of law are not able to hold personal rights, they significantly differ from full persons in law. On the other hand, there is also an essential difference between them and mere objects (things) lacking any subjective interests that could be legally protected. This fact renders the traditional dichotomy used in legal thought since Roman times dividing the reality into objects (things) and persons.[3] Such dichotomy creates a conceptual gap that not only distorts the way in which law grasps reality but leads to increasingly serious moral errors.

---

2 I do not engage here in discussion of more precise criteria of their definition and delimitation. Many interesting insights in this respect may be found in the literature on the idea of "human rights (see e.g. Tasioulas, 2015).

3 "*Omne autem ius, quo utimur, vel ad personas pertinet vel ad res vel ad actiones*" (Gaius, Institutiones, 1.II.8).

6. Towards Modestly Speciesist Account of Personhood

It is within the power of the lawmaker to decide which legal status is conferred on whom. Legislative determinations, however, should be based on empirically informed rational moral reasoning. The overwhelming evidence available today, and its clear ethical implications, provide a sound basis for reexamination of the present approach to personhood in law (even if they remain, to some, relatively narrow, extent, still disputable). This evidence provides compelling reasons to recognize at least some subjective interests of vertebrate animals as deserving legal protection. Therefore, their status should be transformed into non-personal subjects of law capable of holding elementary rights (albeit incapable of having any personal rights) (Elzanowski, Pietrzykowski 2013). This is particularly clear in cases of species displaying astoundingly complex forms of consciousness (including self-consciousness) such as dolphins, primates, and some birds (crows, parrots). The scientific and ethical grounds to reform the legal position of sentient animals are well-known and there is no point in reproducing them here.[4] Instead, I am going to outline my views on the relation of those claims to the status of human beings.

Nowadays, each human being from birth to death is recognized as a person in law. It is one of the crucial axiological foundations of civilized legal systems. It emerged from the long history of atrocities and injustices, based on complete or partial denial of equal status for various groups of human beings regarded as less valuable, and hence, unworthy of full legal recognition. The almost universal acceptance (even if still far from full practical implementation) of equal dignity and status of all human beings should be regarded as an important achievement of the Western legal culture. The painful history should remain a substantial warning for all ideological demands that may adversely affect the quality and level of legal protection enjoyed by each human individual. Therefore, claims to recognize non-personal subjecthood or personhood of non-human creatures should by no means imply depriving any human being of her status. We have to keep in mind the dangers of our fallibility proved by the long list of scientific and moral errors of the past that have led to easy adoption of abhorrent social and legal practices.

As a result, I am inclined to think that a reasonable approach to the reconsideration of moral foundations of personhood in law should remain modestly

4 The scientific literature on the subject is so extensive that it is difficult even to indicate any examples. For review see e.g. Hillix, Rumbaugh 2010). There is also growing philosophical support for the idea of recognition of moral importance of animal subjective good and interests (see e.g. Ch. Korsgaard 2005, 2012, Wolenski 2013).

speciesist. What I mean by that, however, is a deeply reformed and non-exclusive version of humanistic speciesism. It allows for some favor in the treatment of human beings, albeit only relative and by no means excluding the granting of elementary or even personal rights to non-human creatures.

What certainly needs to be overcome is radical speciesism regarding human good as practically the only legitimate goal of the law (or at least strongly preempting any other considerations). There is no metaphysical property making all and only members of the human species intrinsically more valuable than any other actual or possible creatures in the world. We (nor anyone else) do not occupy exclusive, superior position in the moral universe, justifying inherent priority of our interests over all others. Moreover, there is no essential connection between humanness and holding elementary rights. Principally, each creature that is able to possess subjective interests is a potential candidate to be granted elementary rights (insofar as its interests are found to be deserving of protection by means of imposing legal duties on others).[5] Nor is there an essential connection between humanness and personhood. There is only an empirical question whether any non-human creatures possess mental qualities sufficient to have personal rights plausibly conferred (and not only some elementary rights protecting their basic interest). At the moment, the answer to this empirical question still seems negative. Nonetheless, there is nothing absurd or even unrealistic by considering creatures that do not meet (or only partially meet) biological criteria of humanness, but possess capacities enabling them to have any kind of personal rights (Pietrzykowski, 2015b).

On the other hand, a modestly speciesist approach accepts that the criteria applicable to decide about appropriate legal status of human and non-human creatures are different. The legal status of non-human creatures (animals or human-animal hybrids, chimeras, artificially intelligent cyborgs, etc.) should be principally dependent on their actual mental capabilities. Those which are sentient may deserve the status of subjects of law (that is, some of their subjective interests may become legally protected as elementary rights). Their status as persons in law would require evidence that they are able to develop actual mental capabilities enabling them to hold and exercise personal rights.

It is, however, hardly acceptable to apply the same criteria to human creatures. It would result in a serious decrease in level of their legal protection. Many human

5 Additionally, as Ch. Korsgaard rightly points out, most of the relevant duties are primarily collective duties of the politically organized society rather than individual persons in law (see Korsgaard 2014).

beings, e.g. newborns or adults with severe mental dysfunctions would have to be regarded as non-personal subjects of law rather than persons whose rights are exercised by competent custodians (as is the case today). Such conclusions, however, may and should be avoided. The evolution of moral underpinnings of the law should lead to extending rather than shrinking the circle of legal recognition. The concept of non-personal subjecthood may be useful to upgrade the status of the borderline entities, which today are either in an undefined grey area or actually remain deprived of any legal protection whatsoever. In particular, it may concern embryos, pre-implanted zygotes, anencephalic newborns, or human organisms with severely damaged neural structures making them irreversibly unconscious. The intermediate concept of non-personal subjects of law could help to work out more refined and balanced solutions to the problems arising in respect to such kinds of subjects, that seem to not fit either to the category of full persons or mere things.

Regarding human personhood in law, the criteria applicable here should at least allow all human beings to qualify from birth to death (including mentally ill or demented human beings) as persons. Thus, contrary to non-human creatures, the basis to grant personhood to human beings is not the possession of actual mental capacities sufficient to exercise personal rights. It is sufficient for them to be sentient which, in the case of non-human creatures, justifies treating them as non-personal subjects of law capable of holding only elementary rights. A human organism may, in turn, be deserving of the status of a non-personal subject of law, if only it has a potential for developing sentience or has been a sentient creature in the past.

I want to stress, however, that nothing in my argument should be read as an objection against granting non-personal subjecthood or personhood on the basis of similarly extended criteria to any non-human creatures (should there be sufficient reasons to do so). I only oppose such criteria of personhood that would result in significant regress in the legal status that many human beings enjoy today. At the same time, it should not be taken as a reason to obstruct improving and clarifying the legal status of non-human or not-entirely human subjects or even persons (should there appear any).

The approach I argue for is an attempt to reconcile the idea of non-human subjecthood with preserving (if not further extending) the present level of legal protection of all human individuals. Obviously, there is a price of such reconciliation. It is the relative incoherence of the criteria of subjecthood and personhood to be applied to human and non-human creatures. This price seems worthy of being paid in order to avoid obvious moral risks related to actual or potential outrageous consequences of radically specist, as well as radically anti- speciesist accounts of personhood.

7. Two Closing Remarks

Revision of the existing philosophical foundations of the contemporary legal account of personhood is imminent and unavoidable. Such revision is fully justified by moral implications of the contemporary scientific findings. The reasons for such revision will continue to become stronger with further progress of knowledge and technology. Taking this into account, the existing form of radical, exceptionalist juridical humanism is bound to collapse. The theoretical and moral importance of this process makes it necessary to work out and discuss acceptable alternative frameworks. It is the job of legal philosophers, above everybody else, to address these needs.

According to my argument above, the most rational postulate is the evolutionary replacement of the existing form of radically humanistic foundations of the law by its much less exceptionalist version. I dubbed it modestly specist approach to personhood. Nonetheless, even such a change may be hardly achieved without serious refinement of the current conceptual framework present in legal language. Granting elementary rights to non-human creatures implies the distinction between persons and non-personal subjects of law. The need to develop the latter category as something in between persons and things seems obvious and undisputable. It may, in turn, pave the way to further distinction between human and non-human persons (if the latter category will at some moment turn out practically useful).

I would like to stress, however, that even if the morally significant deficiency of the conceptual structure of legal thinking is successfully rectified, it will not eradicate numerous practical problems arising out of real conflicts of interests held by various personal and non-personal subjects of law. The difficulty in solving them could even increase (as some interests that at present are neglected or almost neglected would be upgraded to the status of rights). What then is the point of the postulated revision of the legal approach to personhood? Its main value is to bring the philosophical foundations of the law closer to the moral implications of the contemporary scientific knowledge. Since science and the related evolution of the moral outlook of the world is not about to stall its progress, without such reconsideration the gap between the law and life will continue to widen. Preventing this is by no means trivial.

References

Baker, Lynn R. (2013): *Naturalism and the First-Person Perspective,* Oxford.

Elzanowski, Andrzej, Pietrzykowski, Tomasz (2013): 'Zwierzeta jako nieosobowe podmioty prawa', *Forum Prawnicze* No. 1 (15).

Foot, Philippa (2001): *Natural Goodness*, Oxford.

Hillix William, Rumbaugh Duane (2010) Eds: *Animal Bodies, Human Minds: Ape, Dolphin, and Parrot Language Skills*, New York.

Korsgaard, Christine (2004): 'Fellow Creatures: Kantian Ethics and Our Duties to Animals', *The Tanner Lectures on Human Values,* Volume 25, Salt Lake City.

Korsgaard, Christine (2012): 'A Kantian Case for Animal Rights' In: Michel Margot, Kühne Daniela, Hänni Julia Eds. *Animal Law – Tier und Recht*, Zurich.

Korsgaard, Christine (2013): 'The Relational Nature of the Good', *Oxford Studies on Metaethics*, Vol. 8, Ed. R. Shafer-Landau. Oxford.

Korsgaard, Christine (2014): 'The Claims of Animals and the Needs of Strangers: Two Cases of Imperfect Right' available online: http://www.people.fas.harvard.edu/~korsgaar/CMK.Animals.Strangers.pdf).

Pietrzykowski, Tomasz (2012): 'The Nature and Limits of Conceptual Truths' In: Jovanovic Miodrag, Spaic Bojan Eds. *Jurispridence and Political Philosophy of the XXIst Century.* Peter Lang, Frankfurt a. M.–Bern-Bruxelles-New York-Oxford-Wien.

Pietrzykowski, Tomasz (2015a): 'Rules and Rights' In: Araszkiewicz Michał, Banaś Paweł, Gizbert-Studnicki Tomasz, Płeszka Krzysztof Eds. *Problems of Normativity, Rules and Rule-Following,* Berlin-New York.

Pietrzykowski, Tomasz (2015b): 'Chimery i hybrydy. Podmiotowosc prawna miedzy dogmatem a konwencja' In press. Draft version available online: https://www.academia.edu/11866811/Chimery_i_hybrydy._Podmiotowość_prawna_między_dogmatem_a_konwencją.

Tasioulas John (2015): 'On the Foundations of Human Rights', available online: http://papers.ssrn.com/sol3/papers.cfm?abstract_id=2555277.

White Thomas (2007): *In Defense of Dolphins – The New Moral Frontier*, Oxford.

Wolenski, Jan (2012): 'Podmiotowosc zwierzat w aspekcie filozoficznym' In: Gardocka Teresa, Gruszczyńska Agnieszka Eds.: *Status zwierzecia. Zagadnienia filozoficzne i prawne,* Warszawa.

www.ingramcontent.com/pod-product-compliance
Ingram Content Group UK Ltd.
Pitfield, Milton Keynes, MK11 3LW, UK
UKHW041829100926
8556IPUK00002B/90

9 783631 656853